WordPerfect

Version 6.0

PRISMA Computer Courses are structured, practical guides to mastering the most popular computer programs. PRISMA books are course books, giving step-by-step instructions, which take the user through basic skills to advanced functions in easy to follow, manageable stages.

Now available:

dBase IV
Excel 4.0 for Windows
Lotus 1-2-3
MS-DOS
Novell Netware
UNIX
Windows
WordPerfect
WordPerfect for Windows

Bernd Passens, Ingrid Schöll

WordPerfect

Version 6.0

PRISMA

COMPUTER
COURSE

Prisma Computer Courses first published in Great Britain 1992 by

Het Spectrum
PO Box 2996
London N5 2TA

Translation: George Hall
Production: LINE UP text productions

Reprinted 1994

ISBN 90 274 4181 2

British Library Cataloguing-in-Publication Data.
A catalogue record for this book is available from the British Library.

Contents

Foreword

Word processing is one of the most widely used applications for the personal computer (PC) and WordPerfect is one of the market leaders in this area. There are a number of reasons for this: people often refer to its flexibility and its range of features.

With the arrival of WordPerfect 6.0, the user can now make use of a graphic environment when working under DOS, which makes operation of the program easy and direct. Operating functions which were previously only possible under Windows, are now also available when word processing under DOS:

- commands can be selected using the mouse
- commands can be chosen by clicking on the icons on the toolbar
- pull-down menus provide clarity of choice
- text display can be displayed on screen with all formatting features available.

Here is a summary of what the 6.0 version of WordPerfect enables you to do:

- automatic control of footnotes and endnotes
- move and copy text by means of the mouse (*drag and drop*)
- combine text and graphics in a single document
- format text with lines and boxes
- quick redesign of documents using stored layouts (styles)
- complex series of commands can be stored in a macro and started at one press of a key
- work with extensive column facilities
- apply table and formula functions
- apply mail merge (standard letter) function
- create an attractive presentation of documents by selecting various fonts
- the 'view document' feature displays text and graphics on screen as they will subsequently be printed

- perform a spelling check, use the thesaurus and other utility programs.

If you are not yet familiar with WordPerfect, this book will take you through the program step by step. Advanced users will learn how to use WordPerfect more effectively.

Each chapter starts off by stating its objectives. This will show you what you can expect to have mastered by the end of the chapter. Each chapter also ends with a number of exercises. The layout of the book is such that the early chapters deal with the basic functions (using the keyboard, creating text, editing, saving and printing), while the more advanced features (macros, styles, graphics, text in columns, etc.) are left until you have mastered the basics.

All the examples in this book have been tested with WordPerfect 6.0. Many of them, however, will also work with the earlier versions (5.1 and 4.2).

1 How to use this book

1.1 What hardware do you need?

If you intend working with WordPerfect the minimum requirements are as follows:

Computer:	a computer complying with the industry standard (IBM or similar, compatible computer).
Processor:	the computer must have a 80286 processor or, preferably, higher.
Working memory:	not less than 450 kilobytes of RAM (approx. 450,000 characters) but preferably 520 Kb or more.
Disks:	a floppy disk drive and a harddisk with a capacity of at least 7 Megabyte, but preferably 15 Megabyte.
Printer:	WordPerfect works with almost all current printers.
Monitor:	preferably a colour monitor with graphic possibilities; the computer should possess a graphic card of the VGA, 8514/A or EGA type.

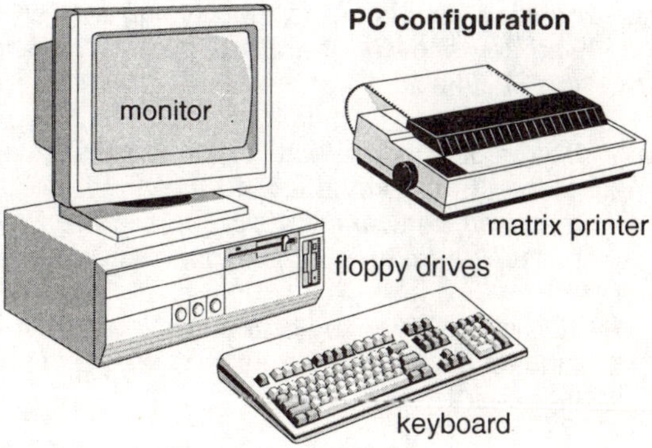

Mouse:	working with the mouse does provide certain advantages in terms of ease of operation.
Operating system:	MS-DOS version 3 or higher.
WordPerfect:	version 6.0.

We shall presume that you are working on a computer which possesses a floppy disk drive and a harddisk and that you have WordPerfect 6.0 at your disposal. Throughout the course of this book, we shall simply refer to WordPerfect.

1.2 The keyboard

1.2.1 General principles

The main keys and what they mean
You use the keys to enter characters or to activate features. The standard IBM keyboard can be divided into three parts:

The alphanumerical part of the keyboard
Most of the keys will be familiar to you from the typewriter. The main ones are:

You can enter capital letters - just as you would on a typewriter - by holding down the key showing an arrow pointing upwards and then typing the letter you want. The key showing the arrow pointing upwards is called the Shift key.

If you want a new line or to confirm a command you press the big key showing the arrow pointing left with the short vertical extension; this is the Enter key (also called Return on some keyboards).

Above the Enter key is another key with an arrow pointing left. This is the Backspace key. Use this key to delete characters.

Alongside the alphanumerical part of the keyboard is the part with operation keys. The Alt key and the Ctrl key are the main ones for WordPerfect. We shall be coming back to these keys later on.

The function keys
Above the alphanumerical part of the keyboard are the function keys (F1 to F12).

Press one of these keys and a feature (function) will be carried out. The significance of the function keys varies according to the program you are using. If you press F10 in WordPerfect, for example, you will start the Save feature.

Number keys and cursor control keys
To the right of the alphanumerical part of the keyboard is the numeric keypad and cursor control keys. These keys allow you to move the cursor (the flashing block). If you want to type a number, you must first press the NumLock key. Press NumLock again to switch it off.

1.2.2 The WordPerfect keyboard template

The **function keys** are used to activate features in WordPerfect. The significance of the keys can be found on a template supplied with the WordPerfect package. This template is illustrated overleaf.

When WP has been started up, you can display this template on your screen by pressing the F1 key twice in succession.

Each key activates **four features**. Therefore twelve function keys provide a total of 48 functions. This is because each function key in WordPerfect can be used in combination with the **Ctrl** key (first function), the **Alt** key (second function), the **Shift** key (third function) or **alone** (fourth function).

	F1	F2	F3	F4
Ctrl	Shell	Speller	Screen	Move
Alt	Writing Tools	Replace	Reveal Codes	Block
Shift	Setup	<-Search	Switch	->Indent<-
	Help/Cancel	->Search	Switch to/Help	->Indent

	F5	F6	F7	F8
Ctrl	Outline	Decimal Tab	Notes	Font
Alt	Mark	Flush Right	Columns/Tables	Style
Shift	Date	Centre	Print/Fax	Format
	File Manager	Bold	Exit	Underline

	F9	F10	F11	F12
Ctrl	Merge/Sort	Record Macro	Tab Set	Save
Alt	Graphics	Play Macro	Table Edit	Envelope
Shift	Merge Codes	Open/Retrieve	WP Characters	Bookmark
	End Field	Save As	Reveal Codes	Block

Look, for example, at what the template shows under key F7.

Notes	Ctrl-F7
Columns/Tables	Shift-F7
Print/Fax	Alt-F7
Exit	F7

On the template these features will appear in various colours if you have a colour monitor.

Notes: Hold down the Ctrl key and press the F7 function key. This enables you to create footnotes, endnotes and comment.

Columns/Tables: Hold down the Alt key and press F7. This activates the Columns/Tables options.

Print/Fax: Hold down the Shift key and press F7. This activates the Print/Fax options.

Exit: Press the F7 key on its own. This will close the current WordPerfect document and lead to the question whether or not you wish to exit WordPerfect itself.

Ctrl key combinations
Frequently-used commands can also be implemented by means of so-called **shortcut key combinations**. These are key combinations which directly activate a specific command. Several of these are listed below:

Ctrl-B	Bold
Ctrl-C	Copy
Ctrl-F	Find Quickmark
Ctrl-I	Italics
Ctrl-O	Outline Edit
Ctrl-Q	Set Quickmark
Ctrl-R	Repeat
Ctrl-T	Toggle text or paragraph number
Ctrl-V	Paste
Ctrl-W	WP Character Sets
Ctrl-X	Cut
Ctrl-Y	Next Window
Ctrl-Z	Undo

These key combinations are activated by first pressing the **Ctrl** key, holding it down and then pressing the letter in question.

The features mentioned will all be explained later in this book.

1.3 Giving commands

Experience has shown that giving commands invariably leads to misunderstandings, so please read the following carefully.

In WordPerfect, commands can be given in **three different ways**:

- by means of the function keys (F1 to F12 or using Ctrl and letter)
- using the mouse or the keyboard in combination with the menus

- using the mouse in combination with the button bar (the button bar is a special bar containing icons which can be activated to implement commands).

For a long time, WordPerfect was the classic example of a program which was operated using function keys. Versions 5.1 and 6.0 brought changes in this field. The structure of the program is now geared to operation by means of menus. But, if you prefer, it is still possible to execute most functions by means of the function keys or Ctrl key combinations.

When working through the examples in this book, we shall presume that you will make use of the menus. You can use both the mouse and the keyboard to do this. Even when you work mainly with the mouse, you will still need to use the keyboard now and again. In that case, keep the following in mind:

- When working with WordPerfect, you often have to press two keys **simultaneously**. The Ctrl, Alt and Shift keys are frequently applied in combination with the function keys. For instance, if you want to centre your text you should press Shift-F6. Hold down the Shift key and press F6. In this book, a hyphen between two keys means that these keys should be pressed simultaneously.

A number of commands are implemented by pressing keys **consecutively**. For example, if you want to move the cursor from the beginning of the text to the end, press the Home key twice in succession and then the Cursor Down key once. In this book when different keys have to be pressed in succession, this is indicated by a comma. For instance, the cursor is moved to the end of the text by pressing Home, Home, Cursor Down.

1.4 The mouse

Although WordPerfect can be operated perfectly well by means of the keyboard, using the mouse makes almost all tasks easier and more straightforward. Accordingly, we shall make a few remarks about how the mouse should be used.

As you would expect, a steady hand is necessary to execute the proper commands when working with the mouse. Each movement of the mouse is converted to movement of the mouse pointer on the screen. The shape of the mouse pointer depends on the current program task. You will use the mouse primarily for moving the cursor, marking (selecting) text and giving commands.

When working with the mouse, three distinctive manoeuvres are performed:

Positioning — Prior to a command being given or any other action being carried out, the mouse pointer must be moved to the appropriate position on the screen. When moving the mouse, do so without pressing any of the mouse buttons. If you cannot see the mouse pointer although you know that the mouse driver program has been installed, make a number of short, quick movements with the mouse. It will probably appear immediately.

Clicking — When you have positioned the mouse at the correct place on the screen, you are ready to give a command. Click on one of the mouse buttons. Press one of the buttons and release it immediately. This is referred to as ‘clicking’. Sometimes you have to click on one of the buttons twice in rapid succession. This is called ‘double clicking’. Normally you only click or double click on the left mouse button.

In this book, if you have to click on the right mouse button we shall explicitly say so, otherwise always click on the left one.

Dragging — This means that you should move the mouse while holding down the mouse button. This also refers to the left mouse button unless explicitly indicated.

The mouse pointer is mainly displayed as a small block when you are working in the text mode and as an arrow when you are working in the graphics mode. These modes will be explained extensively shortly.

1.5 Starting WordPerfect

WordPerfect is started up from the DOS prompt. Check whether the program has been installed correctly on the harddisk. If necessary, first read chapter 15 which deals with the installation of the program and setting the (default) options. We shall presume that the program is adjusted to your system and that your computer has a floppy disk drive A: and a harddisk C:.

Remember, you never work with the program disks themselves, but always with backup copies you have made in advance.

(1) Ensure that there is no diskette in drive A: and switch on the computer, the printer and the monitor.
(2) After a system check, the operating system will be loaded into the computer working memory. As soon as the DOS prompt C:\> appears, this stage has been completed. You may be requested to type the date and time but you can skip these questions by simply pressing Enter twice. A flashing stripe is displayed to the right of the prompt. This is the cursor. This always indicates the position on the screen where commands can be typed or text entered.
(3) The harddisk C: is currently active. The prompt,

C:\> indicates this. Now switch to the directory in which the WordPerfect is stored. This is the directory WP60, so type **cd wp60** (don't forget the space). If WordPerfect has been installed in a different directory, you have to switch to that directory.

(4) If everything has gone smoothly, the C:\WP60> prompt will now be shown.

(5) Start up the program by typing the command **wp** and pressing Enter.

The opening screen should now appear.

Possible errors

- While the computer was being started up, there was a diskette in one of the drives. The operating system has not been loaded properly. Remove the diskette and start up the computer again.
- You are holding the keys down for too long. If you hold the C down too long, for instance, a whole series of Cs will appear on the screen. You can delete the excess Cs with the Backspace key (this is the key with the arrow pointing left, above the Enter key).
- When changing directory (step 3) you have forgotten to type a space between the letters *cd* and *wp60*. Type the command again, but this time with a space.
- Although you have typed the proper command in step 3, an error message appears. In that case, the program has been installed in a different directory. Replace the WP60 directory in step 3 with the name of the directory in which the WordPerfect program is stored. If WordPerfect has been stored in the root directory, you can skip steps 3 and 4.
- You have forgotten to switch on the monitor or the computer. Switch on all the hardware.
- Although the monitor has been switched on (the light is on), the screen remains dark. Check the cable between the computer and the monitor and check the brightness and contrast settings on the monitor.

1.6 The WordPerfect opening screen

When you first start up WordPerfect, you will be asked to enter a licence number. Do that and press Enter. The opening screen appears.

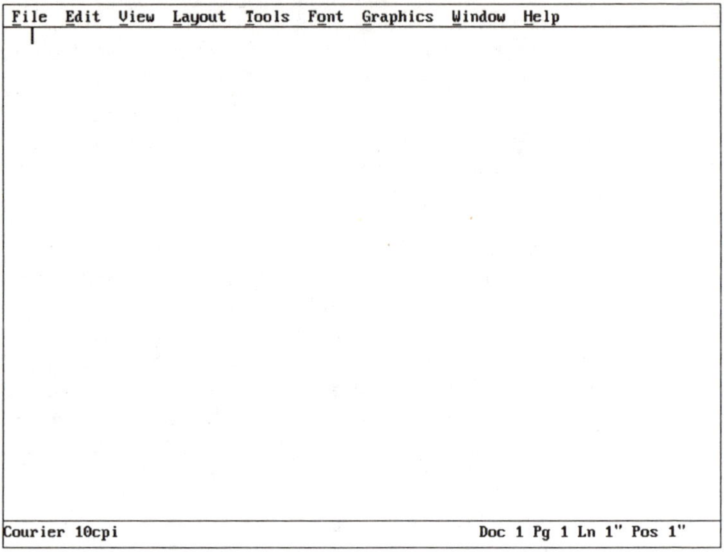

The screen shown here is the screen in the *graphics mode*. If your screen does not look like this (and you would prefer that it did, although this is not really important), press Alt-V. Press Cursor Down so that *Graphics Mode* is highlighted and then press Enter.

The WordPerfect screen is divided into an area for text and an area for information. The largest part of the screen is available for text. The cursor is flashing in the top left-hand corner. This is where you can enter text.

The information area consists of the menubar along the top of the screen and the line at the bottom of the screen, known as the **status line**. This line probably shows (depending on your system settings):

```
Courier 10cpi                 Doc 1 Pg 1  Ln 1"  Pos 1"
```

Courier 10cpi	This means that Courier is the font (letter type) which is currently in use. This font is generally the standard font for most printers.
Doc 1	This indicates that this document is the first of a maximum of nine documents which can be open simultaneously.
Pg 1	The cursor is located on page 1 of the current document.
Ln 1"	The cursor is currently 1" from the top edge of the page.
Pos 1"	The cursor is currently 1" from the left-hand edge of the page.

1.7 Pull-down menus

You can select commands by means of the menus displayed along the top of the screen. Depending on the standard menubar setting, it will be displayed in either the text or the graphics mode. We shall discuss the difference between these two modes shortly. The menubar when in the text mode is shown below:

```
File  Edit  View  Layout  Tools  Font  Graphics  Window  Help
```

The menubar contains nine menus. When you select one of these menus a so-called *pull-down* menu is opened, showing a list of options. You can operate these pull-down menus by means of both the mouse and the keyboard.

1.7.1 Selecting commands using the keyboard

A pull-down menu is opened using an Alt combination. We shall give an example of this below.

(1) Press Alt-F to open the *File* menu.

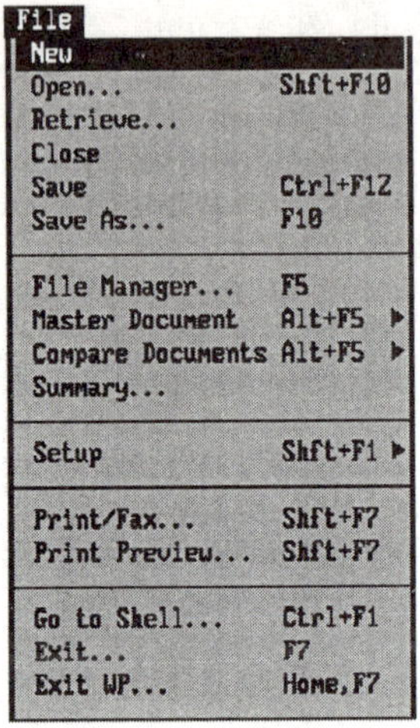

You do not need to remember the letters used in Alt combinations. In the text mode, as here, the relevant letters are shown in a different colour. In the graphics mode, they are shown with underlining.

As the figure shows, an opened menu provides a number of options. You can select the required option by moving to it by pressing the Cursor Down key until it is highlighted. You then actually activate the option by pressing Enter. You can also directly activate the required option once the menu has been opened by pressing the letter which is underlined or displayed in another colour. As an example we shall activate the *Print/Fax* option in the *File* menu:

(2) Press the letter P.

A so-called dialog window appears on the screen. You can specify additional options for the execution of your command (see also section 1.9).

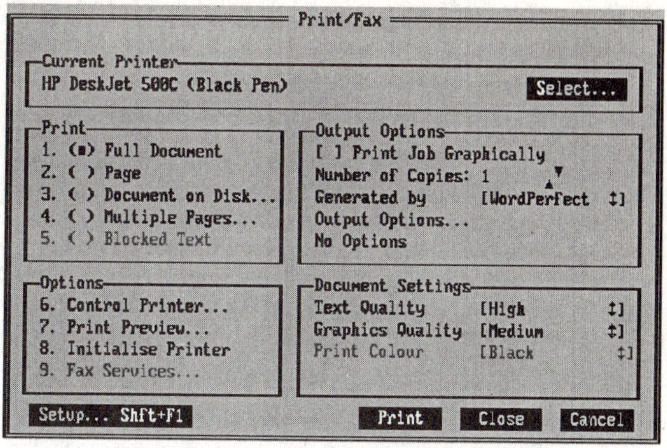

(3) We do not wish to enter any complementary information at the moment so we discontinue the command by pressing the Esc key.

When in a dialog box, you can also move from one option to the next by pressing the **Tab** key.

1.7.2 Selecting commands using the mouse

It is even easier to select commands if you are using the mouse. We shall now select the *Print/Fax* option using the mouse this time.

(1) Move the mouse pointer to the *File* menu.
(2) Click on the left mouse button.
(3) Move the mouse pointer to the *Print/Fax* option in this menu and click on the left mouse button.
(4) Cancel the command by clicking on the *Cancel* button.

Due to the ease of operation we shall use the method with the mouse throughout the rest of this book.

1.8 The Graphics mode and the Page mode

When you start up WordPerfect, the text mode is normally active. WordPerfect works more quickly in this mode, which makes this mode more suitable for entering and correcting texts. The disadvantage of this method is that the text is not displayed on the screen in the same way as it will be printed. If you want to have a screen display which shows text in the form in which it will be printed, you have to switch to the graphics mode.

(1) Select the *Graphics Mode* option from the *View* menu.

The screen display changes and the text is shown in the so-called WYSIWYG quality. This is an abbreviation of *What you see is what you get*. If you open the *View* menu once more, you will see that there is a tick in front of the *Graphics Mode* option. In the *Text Mode*, an asterisk is shown instead.

If you also want to have the page numbers, the headers and footers and the page margins displayed on the screen, select the *Page Mode* option from the *View* menu.

1.9 Working with dialog windows

Some commands are only implemented after you have selected additional options. The communication between user and program takes place via the so-called *dialog windows*. The dialog window which is shown in the graphics mode has a number of characteristic features which we shall outline below.

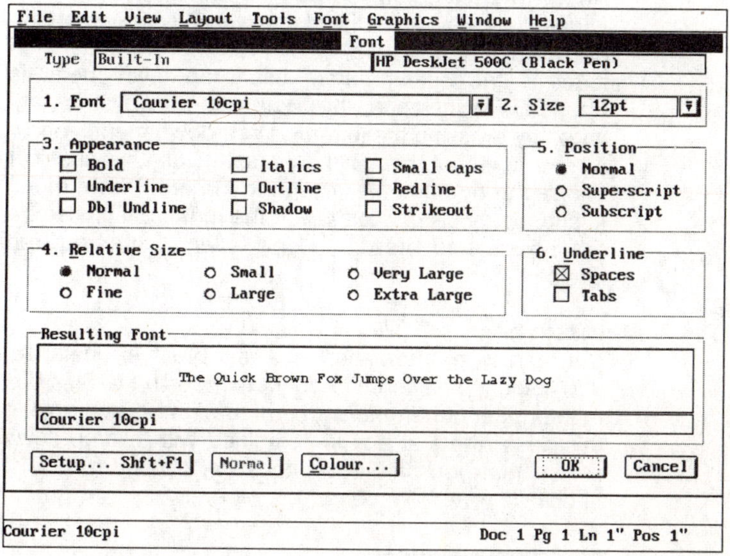

Dialog windows are frequently subdivided into various sections, often separated by frames or borders. In the *Font* dialog window, for instance, these are the sections called Type, Appearance, Relative Size etc. Only the options shown in black letters can be selected, those in grey are not available at the moment.

a) underlined letter
If an option name contains an underlined letter, you can activate this option by pressing the relevant letter. For example, in the *Font* dialog box, you can select the Font option by typing the letter F.

b) check boxes
The small square boxes in dialog windows are called check boxes. Several check boxes can be selected at one time in a certain area. The check box is activated and deactivated by clicking on it. If the option is activated, a cross is shown in the check box.

c) drop-down menus
An arrow pointing downwards indicates that the option in question provides a list of choices. By clicking on the arrow using the mouse, or by pressing the underlined letter in the option name, this drop-down menu is opened. For instance, the Font drop-down list is activated by pressing the letter F. Drop-down menus occur where it is not possible to display all the possible choices at one time. An option in the drop-down menu is chosen by clicking on it with the mouse. It is also often possible to press the first letter of the required choice.

d) text box
You can type information in a text box. For instance, you could type a certain size for the font in the Size box in the upper right-hand corner of the *Font* dialog box. In this case, the text box is combined with a drop-down list so that you can also choose a size from the list shown.

e) example window
The example window, here displayed under the name *Resulting Font*, shows the results of the alterations you have made in the dialog window. In this way, you can examine them before they are implemented. This gives you the chance to experiment with different fonts, appearances and sizes.

f) buttons
Each dialog window contains one or more buttons. The *OK* button for instance is the button used to confirm the alterations you have made in the dialog window. Only then do they come into force. If you click on the *Cancel* button instead, this produces the same effect as pressing **Esc** which means that the dialog window is closed without the changes taking effect.

g) option buttons
In contrast to check boxes, if several option buttons are situated together in one section, only one of these can be selected. The others are then deactivated. The active button is filled in.

1.10 Button bars

It is possible to implement commands quickly and easily in WordPerfect by clicking on the appropriate icon in the button bar. In this way, it is possible for instance to save a document by clicking on the icon showing the words *Save As* under the picture of a diskette. The button bar displayed here is the standard one in WordPerfect. You can determine yourself where the button bar is to be positioned on the screen: Top, Bottom, Left Side, Right Side. This is done by clicking on the *View* menu, and selecting the *Button Bar Setup* option. A dialog box appears in which you can specify the required position.

In addition, it is also possible to alter the standard version of the button bar, which means that you can add special icons to the button bar to represent commands which you yourself often use. It is even possible to compile completely new buttons bars. If the button bar is not displayed on your screen, select the *Button Bar* option from the *View* menu. It will appear along the top of your screen.

2 Getting down to work

In this chapter, we shall deal with the following topics: entering text, correcting and saving it, opening a saved file and printing.

2.1 Entering text

Start up WordPerfect as described in section 1.5. When the opening screen appears, you will know that the program has been started in the proper way. Make the *Graphics Mode* active by selecting this option from the *View* menu. When you begin entering text, pay attention to the following rules:

(1) Unlike the typewriter, when you enter text on the computer you do not need to press Enter at the end of a line to move to a new line. If a word does not fit on the line, it automatically goes onto the next line (automatic word wrap). There are a few exceptions to this rule: you use Enter to make a new line after paragraphs, headings, titles etc. So only press Enter where the text requires a new line.
(2) Do not hyphenate words while you are typing. The words should not be hyphenated until the text has been typed and edited (see also section 6.5).

Normally the hyphenation function in WordPerfect is inactive. If by any chance it is switched on, switch it off again as follows:

(1) Move the cursor to the beginning of the file.
(2) Open the *Layout* menu and select the *Line* option. A dialog window appears.
(3) If the hyphenation option is active a cross will be shown in the check box next to it. Click on this box to remove the cross. The hyphenation function is then switched off.

The dialog box will then look like this:

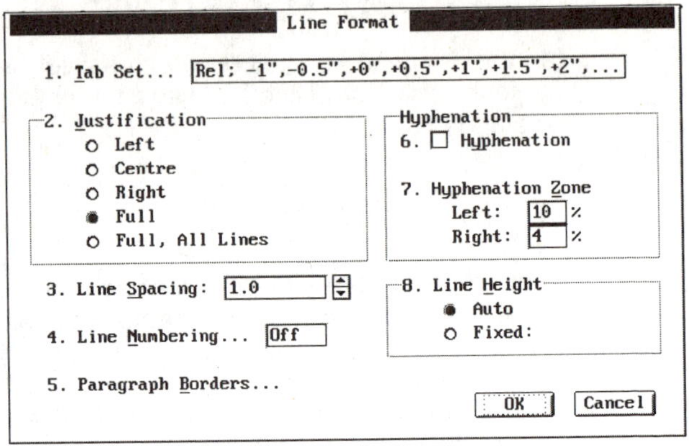

(4) Close the dialog box by clicking on the OK button.

Copy the text below, including typing errors. We are going to use this text to show you how to edit text. If you make any mistakes while you are typing, you can leave them as they are for the moment.

Copy the text below (from *The Hobbit* by Tolkien), including the mistakes. We shall use this text to illustrate how typing errors are corrected. If you make any other mistakes, just leave them as they are for the moment:

> They walkd in single file. The entrance to the path was like a sort of arch leading into a gloomytunnel made by two great trees that leant together, too old and strangled with ivy and hung with lichen to bear more than a few blackened leaves. The path itself was narrow and woubnd in and out among the trunks. Soon the light at the gate was like a little bright hole far behind, and the quiet was so deep that their feet seemed to thump along while all the trees leaned overt them and listened.

> As their eyes became used to the doiness they could see a little way to either side in a sort of darkened green glimmer. Occasionally a slender beam of sun that had the luck to slip in through some opening in the leaves far above, and still more luck in not being caught in the tangled boughs and matted twigs beneath, stabbed down thin and bright before them. But this was seldom, and it soon ceased altogether. There were black squirrels in the wood. As Bilbo's sharp inquisitive eyes got used to seeing things he could catch glimpses of them whisking off the path and scuttling behind tree-trunks. There were queer noises too, grunts, scufflings, and hurryings in the undergrowth, and among the leaves that lay piled endlessly thick in places on the forest-floor; but what made the noises he could not see. The nastiest things they saw were the cobwebs: dark dense cobwebs with threads extraordinarily thick, often stretched from tree to tree, or tangled in the lower branches on either side of them. There were none stretched across the path, but whether because some magic kept it clear, or for what other reason they could not guess.

In order to be able to distinguish the automatic word wrap from the so-called *hard returns* made by pressing Enter, we shall display the hard returns on the screen by means of a special character. Proceed as follows:

(1) Select the *Screen Setup* option from the *View* menu. The following dialog window appears on the screen.

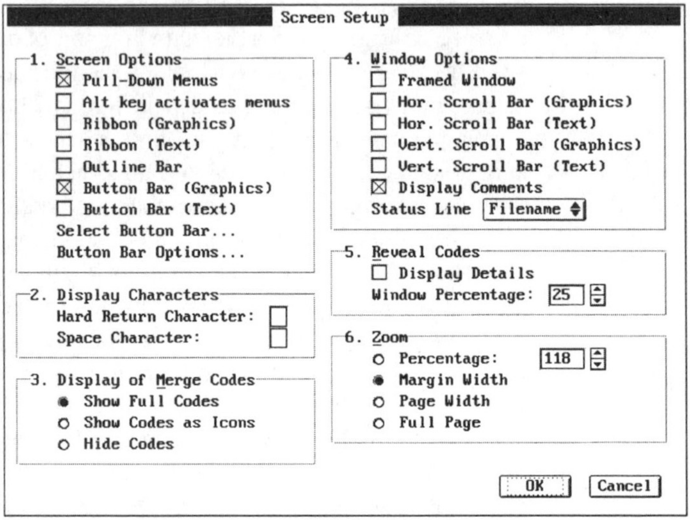

(2) Click in the small text box behind Hard Return Character in section 2. If the text box is empty, the cursor appears here.

(3) Ensure that the NumLock function is activated (the small light will be lit).

(4) Hold down the Alt Key and type the number 20 on the numeric keypad.

(5) The following character should be shown in the text box.

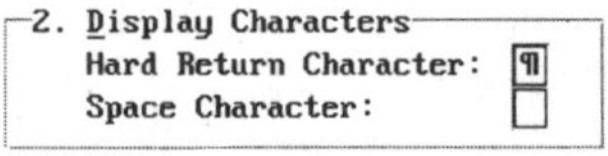

(6) Close the dialog window by clicking on OK.

Those lines which have been ended by pressing the Enter key are now indicated by the specified character. This character is only displayed on the screen; it is not printed.

2.2 Cursor movement

Once you have copied the text we can start correcting the mistakes. To correct a mistake you must first move the cursor to it. You can move the cursor by means of the mouse or by pressing the cursor keys. If you want to move the cursor using the mouse, place the mouse pointer at the required position and click once on the left mouse button. If you prefer using the keyboard, the cursor can be moved by means of the cursor keys and key combinations.

key(s)	**effect**
Cursor Right	one position to the right
Cursor Left	one position to the left
Cursor Up	one line upwards
Cursor Down	one line downwards
Ctrl-Cursor Right	one word to the right
Ctrl-Cursor Left	one word to the left
Plus sign (numeric keypad, NumLock off)	bottom of screen (24 lines)
Minus sign (numeric keypad, NumLock off)	top of screen (24 lines)
PgUp	page up
PgDn	page down
Ctrl-Home, *n*	to page *n* (replace *n* with a number)
Home, Cursor Right	to the end of the line
Home, Cursor Left	to the beginning of the line
Home, Home, Cursor Up	to the beginning of the document
Home, Home, Cursor Down	to the end of the document

Using the *Go to* option from the *Edit* menu or the Ctrl-Home key combination, you can switch to a certain page in one go.

Don't forget: where you see a hyphen press the keys **simultaneously** and where you see a comma press them **consecutively**.

Note
It is generally true of working with word processing that you cannot move the cursor beyond the last character entered. If you want to move the cursor further down without entering text, you can do so by pressing the Enter key.

Important
You cannot move the cursor around a document using either the Enter key or the space bar. By pressing the Enter key you will make a new paragraph and pressing the space bar will produce spaces (empty gaps) in the document.

2.3 Correcting typing errors

WordPerfect normally works in the insert mode. This means that you can later insert letters, words, sentences etc., wherever you want in the document. To do this you must move the cursor using the **cursor control keys** to the place where you want to insert text.

For example: at the beginning of the text is the word 'walkd'. This ought to be 'walked'.

(1) Move the cursor to the d in 'walkd'.
(2) Type an e.

In this way you can insert not only missing letters, but also missing spaces and new lines. Another example. In 'gloomytunnel' there is a space missing:

(1) Move the cursor to the t in 'gloomytunnel'.
(2) Press the space bar.

WordPerfect has a variety of ways to delete text. Here we shall confine the discussion to the Backspace key and the Del key. Other text deletion features will be discussed later. To delete a letter using the Backspace key you must place the cursor **behind** the incorrect letter.

In the text you have typed the word 'woubnd'. The letter b should not be there:

(1) Move the cursor to the letter n in the word 'woubnd' using the cursor control keys.
(2) Press the Backspace key. The letter b is deleted.

There is another way of deleting characters, using the Del key. With the Del key you delete the character at the cursor position when working in the text mode, and the character to the right of the cursor position when you are working in the graphics mode. Correct 'overt them' to 'over them' (we are working in the graphics mode):

(1) Move the cursor to just in front of the t of 'overt'.
(2) Press Del. The character is deleted.

Another way is to use the Ins key. Ins stands for insert. If you press this key it switches off the insert mode and you can delete letters by typing over them.

Example: in the text you have typed 'doiness'. We want to change it to 'dimness':

(1) Move the cursor under the letter o in 'doiness'.
(2) Press the Insert or Ins key. The message 'Typeover' will appear on the status line.
(3) Type the letters i and m. You will see that they replace the letters o and i.
(4) Restore the insert mode by pressing the Insert or Ins key again.

Important
The Backspace key deletes the character to the left of the cursor, while the Del key deletes the character to the right of the cursor position.

2.4 Saving

At the moment your document is not on disk, but is simply stored in computer working memory. This means that if there is a power failure you will lose your entire document. You can only avoid losing it if you store it on disk:

(1) Select the *Save As* option from the *File* menu.

A dialog window appears. If it has no name as yet, it will look like this:

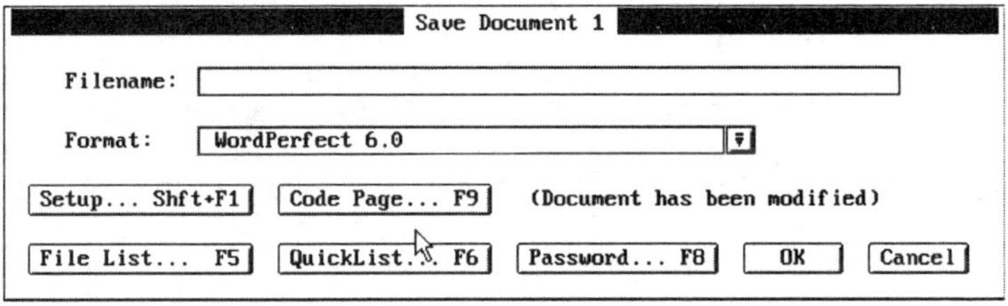

(2) You must now assign a name to this document. The text will be saved on disk under this name. Type *Hobbit*.
(3) Confirm this name by pressing Enter.

Once the computer has finished saving the document, the file name C:\WPDOCS\HOBBIT appears on the status line at the bottom of the screen.

Notes

- Once a document has been saved under a certain name, you can save all further change to the document by selecting the *Save* option from the *File* menu. You can use the Save command as many times as you want because the document is only stored **once** on the disk.
- There is no need for the cursor to be at the end of the document when you save it. The whole document will be saved even if the cursor is in the middle of it.

- Your document will be stored on the disk under a name you have given it, the filename. You can choose whatever name you want, but it is best to choose one by which you can subsequently identify the document.
- A filename may consist of not more than eight letters or numbers or a combination of these. If you want to use more than eight letters or numbers, you can add a point followed by three more characters. For example: HOBBIT.TXT.
- You cannot have any spaces in a filename.
- If you want to save the text on a formatted diskette, select the *Save As* option from the *File* menu. The dialog window shown above appears. Activate the File Name section if necessary by clicking on it and remove the name shown there by pressing the Del or Backspace key. Then type the name A:\HOBBIT to save the text on the diskette in drive A:. Press Enter to confirm.
- WordPerfect will display an error message if the filename you enter does not comply with these rules. You can then retype the name with corrections.

2.5 Finishing work on a file

When you have finished working on a document you can leave it via the Exit feature, F7 or by selecting *Exit* from the *File* menu.

(1) Select the *Exit* option from the *File* menu.
(2) A dialog window appears. You will be asked whether you want to save the text and if so, under its present name or under a different name (*Save As...*).

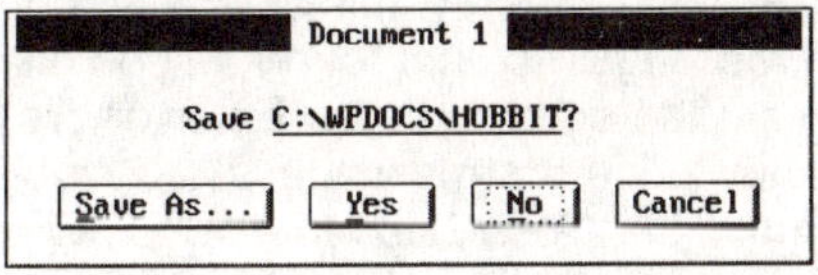

(3) You can also choose not to save the document or to cancel the command so that you can work further on the text.
(4) Click on the Yes button because we do wish to save the document under this name.

2.6 Retrieving an existing document

We do not want to write a new document but retrieve one we have previously saved. This is known as *opening* a document, and is performed, not surprisingly, by selecting the *Open* option from the *File* menu. A total of nine documents can be open simultaneously.

(1) Select the *Open* option from the *File* menu. The following dialog box appears.

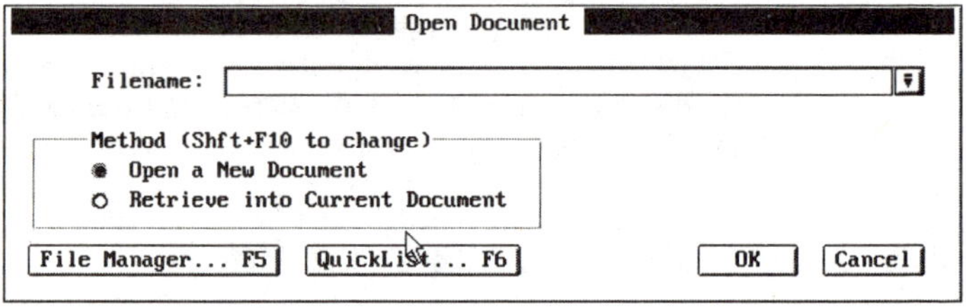

(2) Type the name of the file you want to open in the Filename text box: *hobbit*. If any other characters are shown here you can remove them using the Del or Backspace keys.
(3) Click on the OK button to confirm the command and close the dialog window.

Notes

- If you have made a mistake in typing the name, the message 'File not found' will be displayed in a box on the screen. Press Enter or click on OK to acknowledge the message. Then type the correct name in the *Open Document* window.
- You can also allow WordPerfect to enter the file name. This is done by clicking on the small arrow

pointing downwards at the right-hand side of the Filename box in the *Open Document* window. A list of file names is opened. This list shows the last four texts which were edited. The required file is then opened by double clicking on the corresponding name or by selecting the file using the cursor keys and then pressing Enter.

2.7 Printing the text

You will now want to print your document. We shall assume that you have switched on your printer and the paper is ready. If the text is shown on the screen, select the *Print/Fax* option from the *File* menu.

(1) Select the *Print/Fax* option from the *File* menu or click on the Print button on the button bar. The *Print/Fax* dialog box appears.

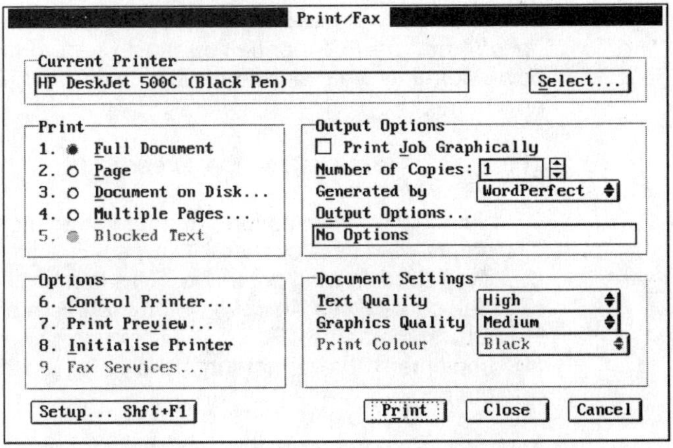

(2) Activate the Full Document option in the Print section. Printing is started by clicking on the Print Button or by pressing Enter since this is the default selection (a dotted line within the button always indicates this).

Possible errors

- The printer will not print. Check that the printer is switched on, that the cables are connected properly and that the printer cover is closed properly.
- The printer must be ready for use. This means in general that the POWER and the ON LINE lights must be on.
- The printer still will not print. It may be that the program has been set for single sheets (sheet feeder) or other settings may not be correct. Check this by controlling the printer (Shift-F7, 6). If the settings look alright, click on the Go button.
- The printer is printing strange characters. This means that the printer has been incorrectly set. Read the instructions in chapter 15 again. Reset if necessary.

2.8 Creating a new text

A new empty window is opened by means of the *New* option from the *File* menu. You must open a new window each time you wish to create a new text under a new name.

The HOBBIT text is still on the screen.

(1) Select the *New* option from the *File* menu. An empty window is opened.
(2) Type the following sentence: 'This is a text.'
(3) Select the *Save As* option from the *File* menu and assign the name TEST.
(4) Implement the command by clicking on the OK button.

Although the HOBBIT text is not visible on the screen, you can edit it any chosen moment without having to open it again.

(1) To edit the HOBBIT text, open the *Window* menu and choose the *Switch To* option. A dialog window appears in which all currently opened documents

are listed. In our case, these are HOBBIT and TEST.

(2) Click on the name HOBBIT in order to switch to that document. You can also return to the TEST document in the same way.

2.9 Exiting WordPerfect

To leave the WordPerfect program, select the *Exit WP* command from the *File* menu.

(1) Select the *Exit WP* command from the *File* menu. The following dialog window appears:

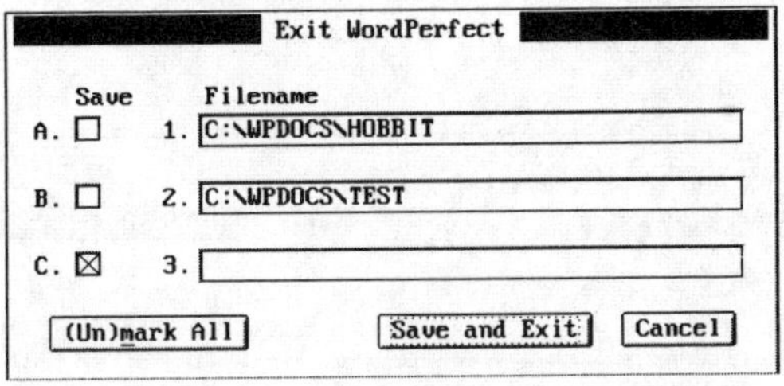

All opened files are shown in the dialog box. The check boxes in front of the filenames contain a cross if alterations to these files have not yet been saved. If you do not wish the alterations in these documents to be saved, remove the crosses in the relevant check boxes by clicking on them. If you have not yet assigned a name to a document, you can do this in the *Filename* box.

(2) Then click on the *Save* or *Save and Exit* button.

Note

Normally, WordPerfect saves opened files automatically every few minutes. You can determine this backup interval by selecting *Setup* from the *File* menu. Then choose the *Environment* option and subsequently *Backup Options*. A cross should be placed in the

Timed Document Backup check box. You can specify the backup interval in the text box underneath. Click on this box, delete the default value using the **Backspace** key and type the number of minutes you wish to apply. Because you can work with nine simultaneously opened files, these backup files receive the names WP{WPC}.BK1 to WP{WPC}.BK9. When WordPerfect is closed by means of the proper command, *Exit WP*, from the *File* menu, these files are automatically deleted. However, if you switch the computer off without closing WordPerfect properly, or if there is a power cut, the following dialog window appears the next time you start up WordPerfect.

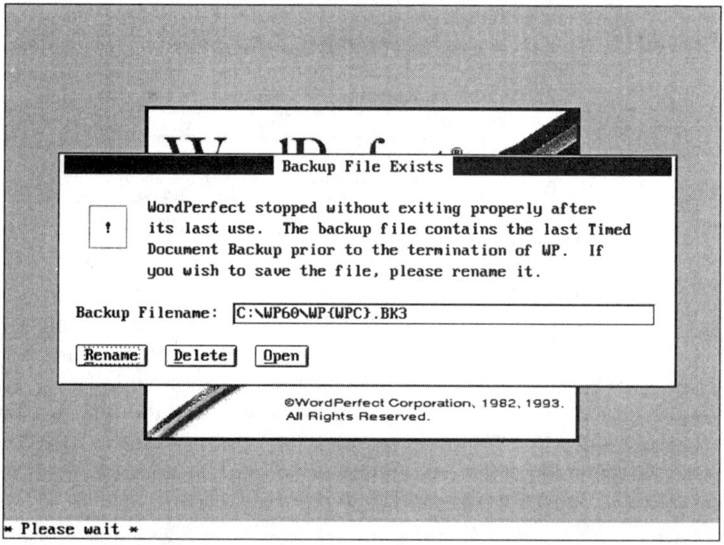

If you click on the *Rename* option, you can specify a different name for the backup file. If you click on *Open*, the backup file is opened. If you click on the *Delete* option, the backup will be removed. If you have made alterations to the file which are not very important since the previous backup was saved, you can select *Delete* here.

This brings us to the end of our first session. In the chapters that follow we shall be taking a closer look at the different steps and the remaining features of the program.

Exercises

Doing the exercises at the end of each chapter will enable you to check whether you have mastered the material in that chapter.

(1) On the screen you see the operating system message C:\>. How should you start the WordPerfect word processing program?

____

(2) What will happen if you select the *Open* command from the *File* menu, type a filename and press Enter?

____

____

(3) You want to save a document for the first time. Write down the command you use to do this and what you would type.

____

(4) You want to move the cursor. How do you do it?
Word by word to the right: ______________
To the end of the document: ______________
To the beginning of the line: ______________

(5) When moving the cursor many beginners make two typical mistakes. What are they?
a) ______________________________
b) ______________________________

(6) You want to correct a typing error. On the screen you have the word Swanstea. You want to delete the t. Where must the cursor be if you want to delete this character with the Backspace key?

____

(7) Which menu command do you use to exit WordPerfect correctly?

____

(8) It is possible to select options in WordPerfect using both the keyboard and the mouse. Which key combination is used to open the *Layout* menu?

____

Answers

(1) *type cd wp60, press Enter*
type wp, press Enter.

(2) *This is the way to open the specified document.*

(3) *Select the Save As option from the File menu. Type the file name, press Enter.*

(4) Word by word to the right: *Ctrl-Cursor Right.*
To the end of the document: *Home, Home, Cursor Down.*
To the beginning of the line: *Home, Cursor Left.*

(5) *a) The cursor is moved with the space bar.*
b) The cursor is moved with the Enter key.

(6) *The cursor must be placed immediately to the right of the t.*

(7) *Via the Exit WP command from the File menu.*

(8) *Alt-L.*

3 Getting Help

This chapter will tell you about the function of the Help key, F3. Once you have read through this chapter you will be able to get information about any WordPerfect feature you want.

There are two ways of obtaining more detailed information in WordPerfect:

- by activating the *Help* menu
- by pressing F1 to obtain context-related help.

Start WordPerfect. As soon as the WordPerfect logo appears on the screen, you know that the program has started properly.

3.1 The first method: the Help menu

You can obtain all kinds of help by opening the *Help* menu.

(1) Open the menu by clicking on *Help* on the menu-bar.

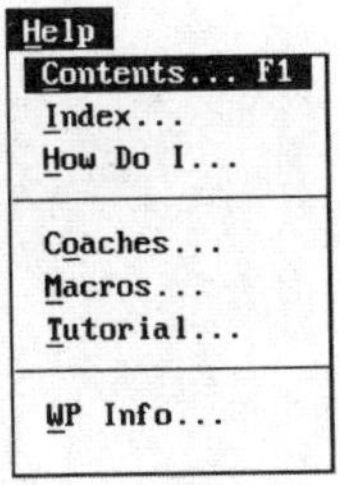

This menu provides the following options:

Contents	Provides a list of frequently-used Help topics.
Index	Provides an alphabetically organized list of various Help topics. Double click on the required topic for more information. When you have read the text, click on the *Contents* button to return to the Contents page of the Help function. Double click on *Index* to return to the Index page. Press Esc to leave the *Help* menu.
How Do I	This option provides an extensive explanation of the most important basic functions of the program.
Coaches	This option opens an interactive tutorial program. In contrast to common tutorials, Coaches provides direct support on the currently active text.
Macros	Provides support when working with macros.
Tutorial	This option starts an interactive tutorial program. In contrast to the Coaches option, Tutorial does not deal with a specific text.
WP Info	Contains information about the current version of WordPerfect.

An example of the *Help* menu in use is shown below. Imagine that we want to gain information about printing a file.

(1) Select the *Index* option from the *Help* menu. The Index page appears.

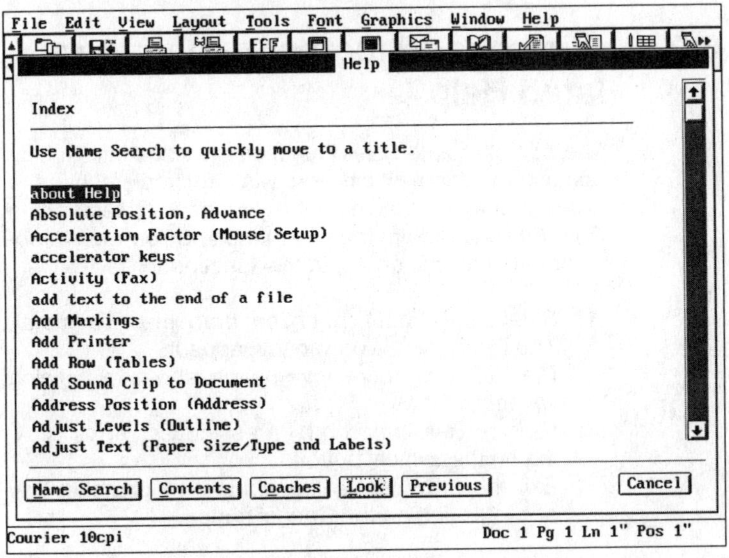

(2) An alphabetically arranged list of Help topics is displayed. Browse through this list using the PgDn key or Cursor Down until you come to the *Print/Fax* option.

(3) Double click on the appropriate line. The page containing information about printing a text and sending a fax appears.

(4) Click on the Cancel button to quit the Help function.

Note
In Help texts there are often references to other topics. If you click on these terms which are shown in bold, a

new Help page will appear. If you click on the Previous button, you will return to the previous Help page. Some terms in the Help texts are underlined. If you double click on these, a brief outline of the corresponding term is shown on the current page.

3.2 The second method: context-related Help

The context-related Help function provides information about a function which you wish to implement at a given moment. Imagine that you have selected the *Print/Fax* option from the *File* menu and you wish to obtain more information about this function.

(1) Select the *Print/Fax* option from the *File* menu. The Print/Fax dialog window appears.
(2) Press F1 for more information about this dialog window.
(3) Exit the Help function by pressing Esc or by clicking on the Cancel button.
(4) Exit the Print/Fax dialog window by pressing Esc or by clicking on the Cancel button.

4 Undoing commands and changes

In this chapter we shall show you how you can exit from features you have unintentionally activated and how you can restore deleted text.

4.1 Undoing commands

You can undo the previous command by activating the *Undo* option from the *Edit* menu. This applies to actions such as deletion or input of text or other commands which lead to alterations in the text (such as selection of fonts or specification of margins).

4.2 Restoring deleted text

Here is an example of how deleted text can be restored.

(1) Type the word 'removal'.
(2) Keep pressing the Backspace key until the whole word has been deleted.
(3) Select the *Undelete* command from the *Edit* menu. The word reappears on the screen in inverse video. In addition, the following dialog box appears:

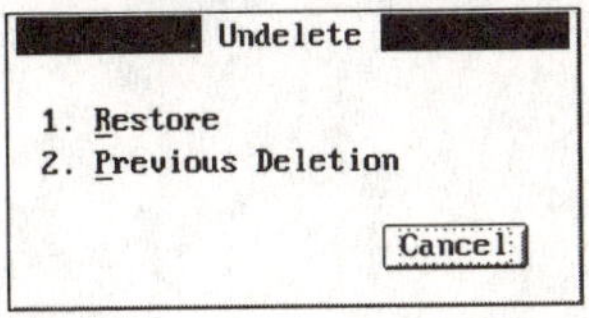

Restore	Enters the displayed text at the current cursor position.
Previous Deletion	Provides the possibility of 'browsing'

	through the previous three deletions. When the required text is shown, restore it to the screen by clicking on Restore.
Cancel	Quit the dialog box without restoring the deleted text.

(4) In this case, we shall choose the Restore option.

Note: In contrast to the *Undo* option from the *Edit* menu, the *Undelete* option always restores a deleted text at the current cursor position.
Example: Imagine that you have deleted a header above a text and have then moved the cursor to the end of the text. If you then select the *Undo* option, the header is restored above the text. If you select the *Undelete* option, the header is placed at the current cursor position which, in this case, is at the end of the text.

Exercises

(1) You want more information about the *Save As* function. How do you gain this information?

____

(2) You want a summary of the operation of the function keys. How to you obtain this?

____

(3) Complete the following: Using the __________ option from the *Edit* menu, the previous ________ deletions can be restored.

(4) Complete: Using the ________ option from the *Edit* menu, the previous deletion can be ________.

Answers

(1) *Select Save As from the File menu and press F1.*

(2) *Select the Contents option from the Help menu and double click on the Template option.*

(3) Using the *Undelete* option from the Edit menu, the previous *three* deletions can be restored.

(4) Using the *Undo* option from the Edit menu, the previous deletion can be *restored.*

5 Editing text

In this chapter we shall be taking a look at the remaining editing features and at one of the features at the heart of WordPerfect: Block. We are assuming that the document stored on the work disk under the name HOBBIT is still on the screen. If this is not the case, you can load the document.

5.1 Other delete features

5.1.1 Deleting words

We want to delete the word 'dimness' in our document and replace it with the word 'twilight':

(1) Move the cursor to the d of 'dimness'.
(2) Press Ctrl-Backspace.
(3) Type 'twilight' followed by a space.

5.1.2 Deleting lines

To delete the first line:

(1) Move the cursor to the beginning of the first line of the document. You need to do this because with this feature the line is always deleted from the cursor position to the end of the line.
(2) Press Ctrl-End (the End key is on the right of your keyboard, in the numeric keypad).
(3) As the cursor is still at the beginning of the line, you can restore the deletion by selecting *Undo* from the *Edit* menu. The original situation is restored.

5.2 Insert

5.2.1 Inserting passages

You can, of course, insert longer passages. In our document we want to insert another sentence:

(1) Move the cursor to just in front of the first letter of the second sentence, 'The entrance to the path...'.
(2) Now type: 'They said nothing.' Type a space after the full stop.
(3) If you look at the screen, you will see that the text has been shifted to the right and wrapped to the following line where necessary.

5.2.2 Inserting and deleting blank lines

We want to insert another blank line between the first and second paragraphs. We shall subsequently delete it again:

(1) Move the cursor to the beginning of the second paragraph ('As their eyes...').
(2) Press Enter. This inserts a blank line.
(3) To delete the blank line again, you must move the cursor to the beginning of the blank line and press Del.

Important: Superfluous indentations and blank lines are deleted just like any other character when using word processing programs. It is important that the cursor is at the **beginning** of the line if you want to remove a superfluous blank line. It may be necessary to press **Del** several times to remove a blank line. This is due to the fact that there are spaces and/or other non-visible characters on the line in addition to the Enter character.

5.3 Working with the block feature

5.3.1 Basic rules

The **block feature** is one of the most important features in WordPerfect. Many operations require that you first mark the piece of text in question using the Block function key. This is what you do: place the cursor at the beginning of the passage you want to mark. Press Alt-F4 to activate the Block feature. Then move the cursor to the end of the text to be highlighted. This can also be done by dragging the mouse over the text to be selected while holding down the left mouse button. The selected text is displayed inversely. Once you have highlighted the passage as a block, you can start the desired operation. Here are a few examples of operations you can execute using the block feature:

- printing
- deleting
- saving
- moving and copying
- making bold and underlining
- centring
- sorting
- changing letter size.

5.3.2 Moving a block of text

By 'move' we mean removing a piece of text from its original position and putting it somewhere else in the document. We are going to put the second paragraph in our practice document in front of the first one:

(1) Move the cursor to the beginning of the second paragraph, in our case the letter A of 'As their eyes...'.
(2) Press the left mouse button and hold it down.
(3) Drag the mouse pointer downwards until the whole paragraph is selected. If you mark too much text, you can unmark the extra section by dragging the mouse pointer across the extra section.

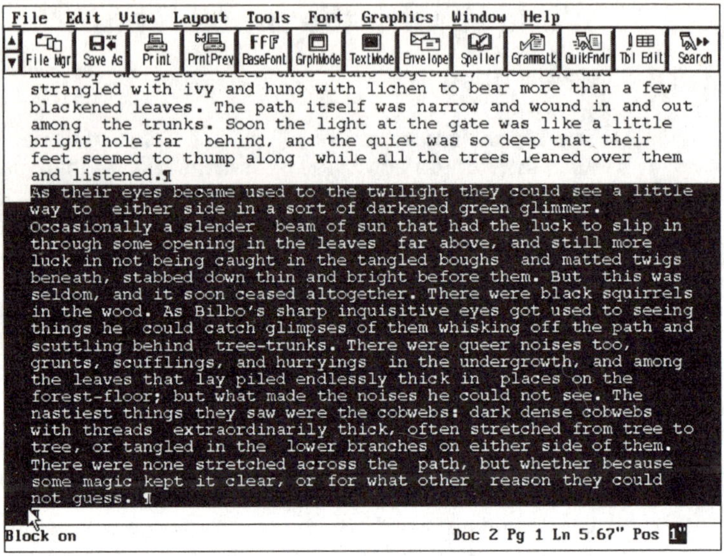

(4) Select the *Cut* option from the *Edit* menu or press the key combination Ctrl-X. The text disappears from the screen.

(5) Now move the cursor to the position where the marked text is to be situated. In our case, we wish to move this text to the beginning, so press the combination Home, Home, Cursor Up.

(6) Select the *Paste* command from the *Edit* menu. The text reappears on the screen at the required position.

Notes

- When you have selected a section of text by holding down the mouse button, the message 'Block on' is shown in the status line at the bottom of the screen.
- If you wish to unmark a block, click on a random place in the text.
- There are several functions which can be activated by means of the mouse:

mouse operation	**result**
Double click on a word	Select the word.
Click three times on a text position	Select the sentence.
Click four times on a text position	Select a paragraph
F12, Shift-Click	Select the text from the cursor position to the mouse pointer.

- Those preferring to work with the keyboard should proceed as follows:

(1) Place the cursor at the beginning of the text to be marked.
(2) Press Alt-F4 or F12.
(3) Move the cursor to the end of the text to be marked. If you type any character, WordPerfect will mark the text up to and including the first occurrence of that character. This need not be a letter; it may also be a space, an Enter sign or a punctuation mark. In our case, we could have selected the paragraph as follows:
    a) Place the cursor at the beginning of the text.
    b) Switch on the block function by pressing F12. The words 'Block on' appear on the status line.
    c) Press Enter. The text is selected up until the first Enter sign. Press F12 once more to switch the block function off.

- It is also possible to select a paragraph, a sentence or a page by means of the *Select* option in the *Edit* menu. Place the cursor in the appropriate text section before choosing this command. Subsequently choose the required option from the submenu which appears.
- Sections of text can also be moved using the so-called *drag and drop* method. When you have selected the relevant section of text, click using the mouse in that text section and hold the mouse button down. Then drag the section to the required

position. As soon as you release the mouse button, the text appears at the new position.

5.3.3 Copying a block of text

When you copy text the highlighted block does not disappear from the screen as it does when you move text, but stays in its original position and **also** appears in another position.

We are going to copy the paragraph from 'As their eyes...' to 'he could not see.' to the end of the document:

(1) Place the cursor in this paragraph.
(2) Select the paragraph by choosing the *Select* option from the *Edit* menu. Choose the *Paragraph* option from the submenu.
(3) Select the *Copy* command from the *Edit* menu.
(4) Place the cursor at the end of the text. The quickest way of doing this is to press Home, Home, Cursor Down.
(5) Insert the copied text at the new position by means of the *Paste* command from the *Edit* menu.

Note
Sections of text can also be copied using the *drag and drop* method. When you have selected the text, click in the selected text section while holding down the **Ctrl** key. Hold down the mouse button and the Ctrl key and drag the mouse pointer to the required position. As soon as you release the mouse button and the Ctrl key, the section of text appears at the new position.

5.3.4 Deleting a block of text

The paragraph we have just copied to the end of the document is, of course, superfluous. We shall therefore delete this paragraph again straightaway.

(1) Move the cursor to the beginning of the last paragraph and select it using the *Select* option (and then *Paragraph*) from the *Edit* menu.
(2) When the paragraph has been selected, press the Del key.

Note
You can retrieve the text by means of the *Undo* or *Undelete* option from the *Edit* menu if you accidentally delete the wrong piece of text.

Exercises

(1) Give the key combination for the function which deletes a word to the right.

____

(2) You want to highlight a complete document as a block. The cursor is at the beginning of the document. Give the full key combination.

____

(3) Name at least three operations you can do in combination with the Block feature.

____

____

____

(4) You have accidentally marked a section of text using the mouse. How do you unmark it again?

____

Answers

(1) *Ctrl-Backspace.*

(2) *F12, Home, Home, Cursor Down.*

(3) For example: *Print Block, Move Block* and *Delete Block*. Other features are listed in section 5.3.1.

(4) *By clicking with the mouse in or outside the marked text.*

6 Basic text formatting features

In this chapter we shall be taking a closer look at the text formatting features available, such as bold text, underlining, placing letters above or below the line and changing the margins. WordPerfect has a number of powerful tools for formatting text, such as the use of tabs and display of codes.

6.1 Underlining and bold

6.1.1 As you type

When working with WordPerfect you can display the letters underlined or made bold as you type, but you can also edit sections of text later. If you wish to use the first method, proceed as follows:

(1) First select the *Bold* or the *Underline* options from the *Font* menu. A tick is placed in front of the activated option.
(2) Type the piece of text you want bold or underlined.
(3) You can switch the Bold and Underline features off again by selecting them from the *Font* menu. The tick is removed.

In WordPerfect underlined and bold text will appear as such on the screen. If the bold and underline features are not displayed on the screen, this probably means that you are working in the text mode. Switch to the graphics mode in the *View* menu. In other words, the asterisk is removed from the text mode option.

As an example we shall demonstrate underlining. You make text bold in a similar way. If you do not have your practice document on the screen, load it by selecting the *Open* command from the *File* menu. Type HOBBIT in the Filename box and press Enter. Go to the end of the text by pressing Home, Home, Cursor Down. Then proceed as follows:

(1) Activate the *Underline* option from the *Font* menu.
(2) Type: 'It was not long before they grew to hate the forest as heartily as they had hated the tunnels of the goblins'.
(3) Switch the Underline feature off again by selecting *Underline* in the *Font* menu once more.

6.1.2 Existing text

If you want text you have already typed to be made bold or underlined, you must first highlight the text in question as a block.

(1) Highlight the word 'Occasionally' in the first paragraph using the Block feature, Alt-F4.
(2) Select the *Bold* option from the *Font* menu.

You underline existing text in a similar way.

6.2 Deleting underlining and bold

6.2.1 Reveal codes

We can of course also change bold and underlined text back into normal text. Before explaining how to go about this, we must first turn to the Reveal Codes feature.

WordPerfect makes a distinction between entering text and entering codes. All the codes you enter are stored just like the text. The difference is that the codes do not appear on the screen, while the text does. However, you can display these codes by selecting *Reveal Codes* from the *View* menu (the shortcut key combination is Alt-F3). If you want to use this key, you must move the cursor to the point in the document where you activated a feature. Then select *Reveal Codes* from the *View* menu (or press Alt-F3). The screen is divided into two parts. While the document appears in its normal form in the upper part of the screen, in the lower part it appears with the associated codes.

An example: we want to display the codes for the Underline feature:

(1) First move the cursor to the position at which you activated the feature. As we underlined a section of text at the end of the document, we shall move the cursor to there. ('It was not long...').
(2) Activate the Reveal Codes feature by pressing Alt-F3.
(3) You will now see the following on the screen:

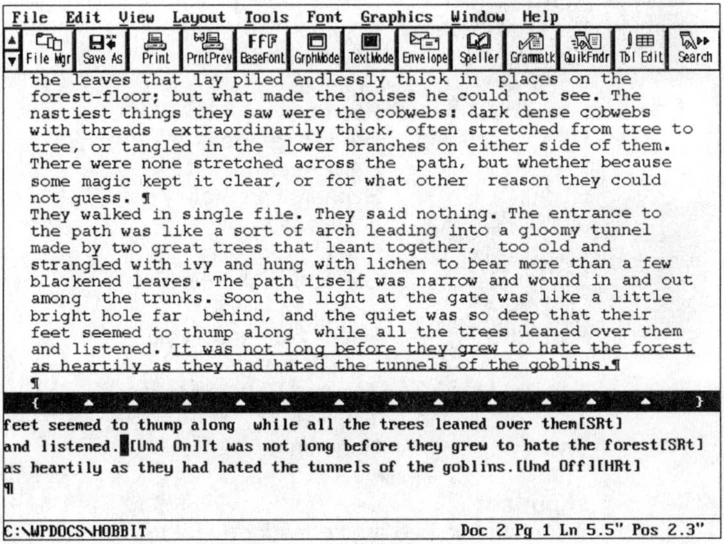

(4) The screen is divided into two by the Tab Ruler.

We shall look first at the bottom part of the screen.

The sentence starting with 'It was not long...' is wedged between the codes **[Und On]** at the beginning of the relevant text and **[Und Off]** at the end of it.

(5) Switch off the Reveal Codes feature by selecting *Reveal Codes* from the *View* menu. The normal screen will reappear.

Summary of the main codes and what they mean:

code	**meaning**
Block	Beginning of Block
Block Pro	Block Protection
Bold	Bold
Cntr Pgs	Centre Pages (Top to Bottom)
Cntr on Cur Pos	Centre on Current Position
Col Def	Column Definition
Date	Date/Time Function
Dec Tab	Decimal Tab
Dbl Und	Double Underline
Endnote	Endnote
Footnote	Footnote
HPg	Hard Page Break
HRt	Hard Return
Hyph	Hyphenation State
Just	Justification
Lft/Rgt Indent	Indent
Lft/Rgt Mar	Left and Right Margins
Lft Tab	Left-aligned Tab
Paper Sz/Typ	Paper Size and Type
SRt	Soft Return
Top/Bot Mar	Top and Bottom Margins
Tab Set	Tab Set
Und	Underlining

Important
If you want to see the codes for a feature you have activated on the screen, **first** move the cursor to the position where you activated the feature and then select *Reveal Codes* from the *View* menu. Since the Reveal Codes feature shows almost every command, you may find the screen presentation of the codes rather unclear if you activated several features in the same place.

6.2.2 Deleting codes

It is convenient to know how to reveal the codes you have placed in a document because nearly all the features you can activate while working with WordPerfect can be cancelled by deleting the relevant code.

For example: we want to remove the underlining in the sentence, 'It was not long before they...':

(1) Move the cursor to the beginning of the line.
(2) Activate *Reveal Codes* from the *View* menu by pressing Alt-F3.
(3) Now move the cursor to the right of the code **[Und On]** using the cursor control keys.

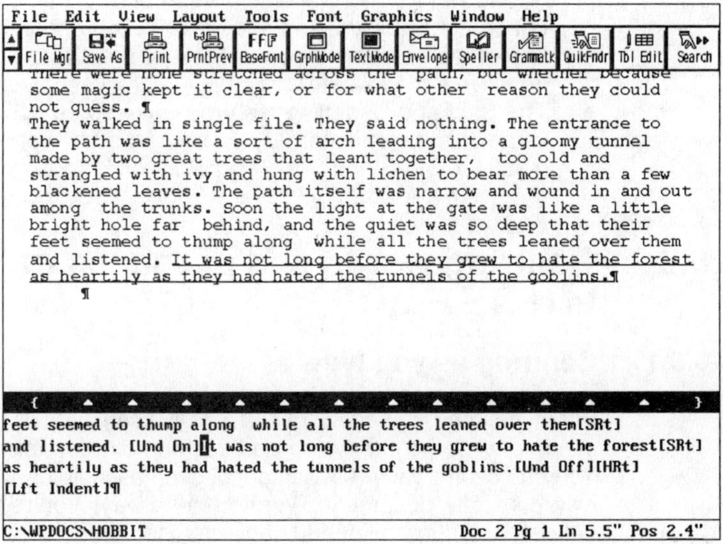

(4) Delete the code using the Backspace key.
(5) Switch off the *Reveal Codes* feature by selecting it again from the *View* menu or by pressing Alt-F3 again.

The Underline feature has now been cancelled. On the screen the line appears in normal script again. You can do the same with any bold words in the document.

Important
To cancel the codes for bold text, underlining etc., you only need to delete one of the two codes, in other words either the one at the beginning or the one at the end of the passage of text.

Remarks

- The *Reveal Codes* function can be activated from the *View* menu, or by pressing Alt-F3 or F11. This is a matter of personal preference.
- Some commands can only be undone in the Codes window. However, the *Bold* and *Underline* options in the *Font* menu work as switch options. Select the required section of text and activate or deactivate the relevant option.
- The Bold and Underline features can also be activated (and deactivated) by pressing the key combinations Ctrl-B and Ctrl-U respectively.

6.3 Centring words and passages of text

6.3.1 Centring as you type

When centring, we must make a distinction between centring while we are typing and centring existing text. You can centre a word, a sentence, even a whole page or a complete document. WordPerfect always centres between the current left and right margins.

To illustrate this, we want to insert a centred title at the beginning of our document:

(1) Move the cursor to the beginning of the document (Home, Home, Cursor Up).
(2) Make two blank lines by pressing Enter twice.

(3) Then move the cursor up to the top blank line by pressing Cursor Up twice.
(4) Select the *Alignment* option from the *Layout* menu. In the submenu which appears, select the *Centre* option.
(5) The cursor will jump to the middle of the line.
(6) Now type 'Flies and Spiders'.
(7) When you have finished typing, conclude by pressing Enter.
(8) The cursor will jump to the beginning of the next line. This simultaneously concludes the Centre function.
(9) Activate the Reveal Codes feature by pressing F11. Switch Reveal Codes off again by pressing F11 once more.

6.3.2 Centring existing text

If you want to centre a passage of text after typing it, you must first highlight the passage. Convert the final sentence of the document into a paragraph by moving the cursor to just in front of the word 'It' and pressing Enter.

(1) The cursor is located at the beginning of the sentence 'It was not long...'.
(2) Activate the Block feature by selecting the *Select* option from the *Edit* menu. Choose Sentence from the submenu by clicking on it.
(3) Now select the *Alignment* option from the *Layout* menu and click on Centre.

In this case too, you can undo this action by removing the code at the beginning of the section of text.

Remarks

- Instead of using the menu command, you can press the key combination Shift-F6 to centre a section of text.
- It is also possible to centre a section of text by means of the Centre button on the Ribbon. The

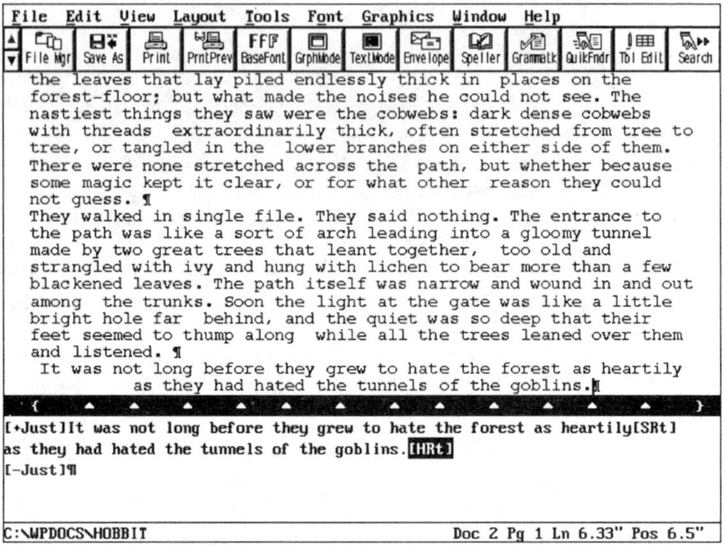

Ribbon is a slender bar above the Toolbar. It contains a number of basic functions for determining the size and appearance of the text. If the Ribbon is not shown on your screen, you can activate it by clicking on the name in the *View* menu.

6.4 Margins and line spacing

6.4.1 Changing margins

You can use the *Margins* option from the *Layout* menu to alter the default page layout settings. The default left and right margin settings in WordPerfect are 1 inch, in other words, a margin of 1 inch is left unused at the left- and right-hand sides of the text. If you want to change these settings, you must remember that any changes you make will apply **from the position at which you make them**, that is, from the position where you chose the *Margins* option in the *Layout* menu.

In our practice document we want to leave the left margin as it is and change the right margin to 1.5". If you do not have the document on your screen, load it by selecting the *Open* command from the *File* menu.

(1) Since we want the new margin to apply to the whole document, we move the cursor to the beginning of the document by pressing Home, Home, Cursor Up.
(2) Select the *Margins* option from the *Layout* menu. The Margin Format dialog box appears on the screen.

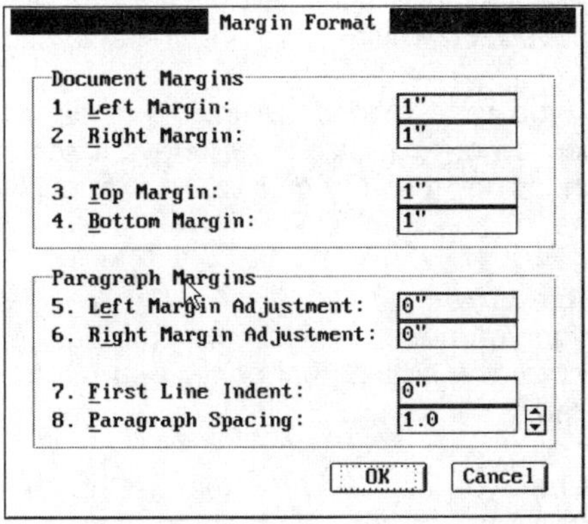

You can specify the four document margins here and also the margins for a selected paragraph.

(3) Click using the mouse in the Right Margin text box in the Document Margins section. Remove the value there by pressing **Del** and then type 1.5. Click on OK.

The text is immediately shown on the screen with its new margin settings.

You can always remove the new settings by opening the Reveal Codes screen (F11) and deleting the appropriate code there. This is done by moving the cursor to the **[Rgt Mar]** code. When the cursor is positioned there the new value is displayed. Then press the **Del** key. The text acquires the default format.

Remarks

- A margin change need not apply to the whole document. You can activate the feature anywhere you want in the document. You must be sure, however, that the cursor is at the beginning of a line when you do so. If you activate the feature in the middle of a line, WordPerfect will make a new line at the cursor position. This setting remains valid until a new setting is specified or the current setting removed in which case the default setting takes over.
- If you wish to change the margins for a certain section of text, select the relevant section prior to choosing the *Margins* option from the *Layout* menu.

Possible errors

Although you have changed the Left/Right Margin settings correctly, nothing happens. Two things may have occurred:

- When you activated the feature the cursor was at the wrong position, at the end of the document instead of at the beginning, for example. In such a case the feature will have no effect on the format of the document.
- You may have forgotten to delete the former margins stored in the document. If you activate the Reveal Codes feature, you can see whether there are any unwanted margin setting codes in the document. Once you have deleted the superfluous codes, the new margin settings will take effect.

6.4.2 Changing line spacing

The same rules apply to this feature as to changing the left and right margins. The default line spacing setting is one. You can change the line spacing at any time and set it to one-and-a-half, two, three and so on. You can also have different line spacings within a single document. Before activating the feature all you need to do is move the cursor to the position from which you want the new line spacing to apply. In our practice document we want to change the line spacing from one to one-and-a-half:

(1) Since we wish the new line spacing to apply to the whole document, we shall move the cursor to the beginning of the document by pressing Home, Home, Cursor Up.
(2) Select the *Line* option from the *Layout* menu. The *Line Format* dialog window appears.
(3) Go to option 3, Line Spacing and replace 1.0 with 1.5.
(4) Click on OK to confirm your specifications.

The text is now displayed with much more space between the lines. This setting will apply until you alter the settings again.

Note: If you wish to alter the line spacing for only a certain section of text, select that section of text prior to choosing the *Line* option from the *Layout* menu.

6.5 Hyphenation

If the Hyphenation option is not on, WordPerfect automatically wraps words extending beyond the right margin setting onto the next line. The result of this, however, is that the right margin becomes very ragged; and where text is justified, very large gaps appear between the words. By activating the Hyphenation feature you can give your document a more attractive appearance.

The default settings (*File* menu, *Setup, Environment*) determine the way WordPerfect splits words. In fact, normally the Hyphenation function is not active in the English version of WordPerfect. If you wish to activate it, Select *Line* from the *Layout* menu and click on the check box to place a cross there. You yourself can indicate when words are to be split by specifying the Hyphenation Zone in the Line Format dialog box (*Layout* menu, *Line*). This determines just how lengthy words have to be before they are split.

WordPerfect has a special program which ensures that words are split correctly. We shall examine the settings.

(1) Select the *Setup* option from the *File* menu and then choose *Environment*. The following dialog window appears:

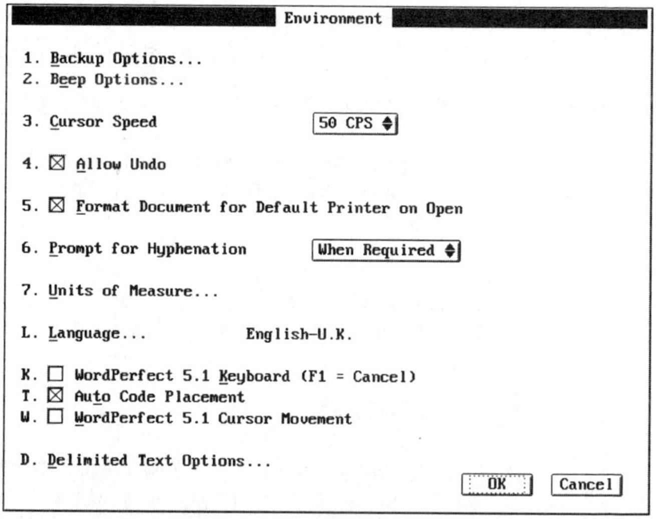

(2) The Language section enables you to specify whether or not WordPerfect should use the UK English language module when applying hyphenation. This is the default setting.

(3) The Prompt for Hyphenation section enables you to specify how and when you wish to support the program in the hyphenation process. If you choose Never, all hyphenation will occur fully automati-

cally. If you choose When Required (the default setting), hyphenation will also take place automatically but the program will interrupt the hyphenation if no rules for a certain word are found. In that case, you will be asked to make the decision. If you select the Always option, you will be asked to confirm or specify each individual hyphenation. Although the When Required option is generally the most convenient option, we shall select the Always option here, just for practice.

(4) Click on Prompt for Hyphenation or press P. Click on Always.

(5) Click on OK to confirm your choice.

Important

All alterations made via *Setup* in the *File* menu remain in force even after the computer has been switched off. This means that they are also in force when the computer is again activated the next time. If you want to restore the original settings, select the When Required option again when you have completed the following exercise.

We presume that the HOBBIT text is still on the screen. If not, open it and go to the beginning of the text by pressing Home, Home, Cursor Up. Switch on the Reveal Codes feature by choosing this option from the *View* menu.

Hyphenation consists of two phases. In the first phase you have to switch hyphenation on. Only then can you start to hyphenate the individual words.

(1) Select the *Line* option from the *Layout* menu.

(2) Activate the Hyphenation box by clicking on it and close the dialog window by clicking on OK. As soon as a word is found which need to be split (in this case 'Occasionally'), a dialog box appears.

(3) If you click on the first option, Insert Hyphen, the word will be hyphenated in the place shown by

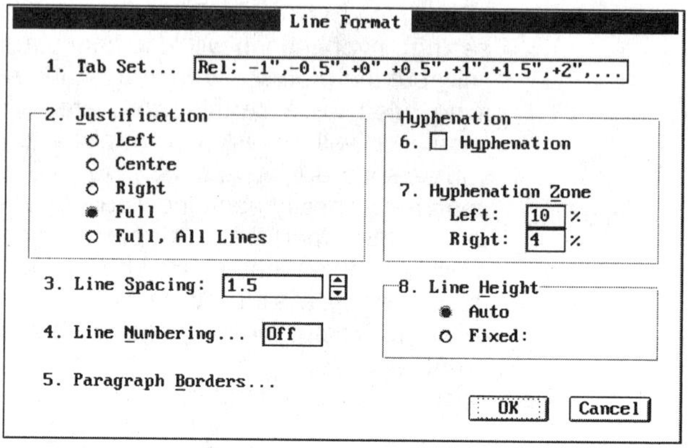

WordPerfect. If you are not happy with the position of the hyphen, you can change it by clicking on the Right Arrow or Left Arrow keys and then selecting Insert Hyphen. If you do not want to have a particular word split, select Ignore Word. In that case, the entire word is wrapped to the next line. If WordPerfect meets this word again in this document, it will again wrap it to the next line.

(4) The program will move through your text asking you to specify the positions of the hyphens. Do this according to your judgement. When there are no more suggestions from WordPerfect, this means that the hyphenation process is complete. You can print the document if you wish.

(5) Since you might find hyphenation a nuisance in the exercises that follow, we shall delete the Hyphenation On code at the beginning of the document again. Move the cursor to the beginning of the document, activate the Reveal Codes feature by pressing Alt-F3 and delete the code [Hyph On].

Notes

- With long documents in particular it is a problem that the words to be hyphenated are taken out of context during hyphenation and displayed as isolated words on the status line. It is thus impossible during the hyphenation process to imagine what the hyphenation will look like when the word is back in the document.

- You can also hyphenate words yourself without switching on hyphenation. Press Ctrl and the dash simultaneously. Never use the dash on its own to hyphenate a word, as all you will be doing is inserting a dash and not a hyphen. Hyphens only appear where there is no more text on the right. If a hyphenated word ends up in the middle of a line as a result of changes in the text or text being inserted, the hyphen will not be visible on the screen, nor will it be printed. Dashes on the other hand are always visible on the screen.
- Incorrect hyphenation can be erased just like any other character. Move to the hyphen and delete it using Del. If the Hyphenation function is active, a new suggestion may be made concerning splitting the word. Specify a new position or place the entire word on a new line by selecting Ignore Word. It is only possible to work in this way if the Always or When Requested options have been activated in the *Environment* window of the *Setup* option. If Never has been activated, it will not be possible to remove the hyphenation. It is then only possible to make corrections when the Hyphenation function has been switched off.
- If not all of the possible splitting positions are shown, move the cursor to the end of the text. All suggestions should now be shown on the screen.
- If you find that there is too much or too little hyphenation in WordPerfect, you can alter the range of the Hyphenation Zone. If this zone is smaller, more words will be split, and vice versa. The hyphenation zones are constructed as follows:

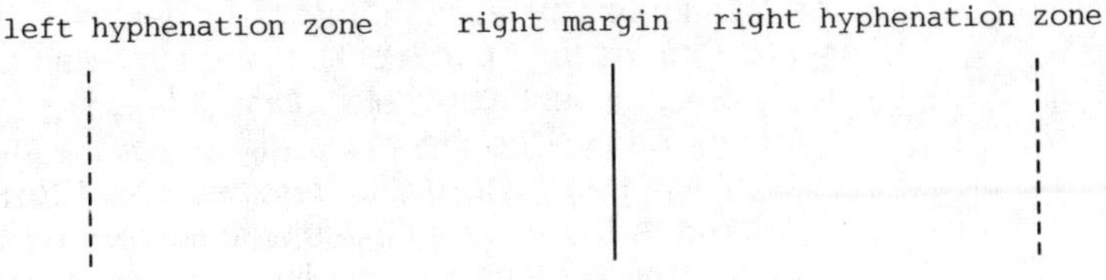

Imagine that you think that there should be more hyphenation because good paper has become very expensive and you want the text to be as compact as possible. Proceed as follows:

(1) Place the cursor at the position where the new hyphenation settings should apply.
(2) Select the *Line* option from the *Layout* menu.
(3) Alter the default settings for the Hyphenation Zone to Left: 3%.
(4) Close the dialog window by clicking on OK.
(5) Move the cursor to the end of the text. You will notice that more hyphenation has been applied.

6.6 Indenting

When you want to indent a passage of text on the typewriter you may be accustomed to using the space bar. In word processing, however, you cannot use it for this purpose. Like many other word processing programs, WordPerfect has a special feature for indenting text. WordPerfect always jumps from the cursor position to the next tab stop. The default tab setting (beginning at 1") is one every half inch (in other words, at 1.5", 2", 2.5" etc.). You can use the indent feature as you type and to edit existing text. The indent continues to apply until a hard return, in other words an Enter character, appears in the text. We want to indent the second paragraph in our practice document:

(1) Move the cursor to just in front of the first letter of the second paragraph.
(2) Indent the line by selecting the *Alignment* option from the *Layout* menu. Then select *Indent ->* from the submenu. This ensures that the indentation is made from the left margin only. If you also wish to apply a right indentation, select *Indent -><-*.
(3) You can remove the indentation by removing the code at the beginning of the indented line. Press F11 to open the Reveal Codes screen. Move the cursor to the beginning of the line and delete the

indent code. The text jumps back to the beginning of the line.

Remarks

- You can indent text from the cursor position to the next tab stop. This means that you can increase or reduce the indentation distance by changing the default tab setting.
- Instead of selecting the *Alignment* option from the *Layout* menu, you can also indent text by pressing the F4 function key. If you wish to indent text on both the left- and right-hand sides, press Shift-F4.

6.7 Working with tabs

The use of tabs can sometimes make the appearance of a document very much clearer. Tabs are fixed points on the screen which you can use by pressing the Tab key or the F4 key (indent). Tabs are particularly useful for the clear arrangement of information in tables, such as columns of figures.

We shall practise using the tab feature with a new document. First clear your screen. If the practice document is still on the screen, you can remove it by selecting *New* from the *File* menu. We presume that the settings in your program are in inches. If not, change this by selecting *Setup* from the *File* menu and then *Environment*. Click on *Units of Measure* in the subsequent list.

Area of each country in millions of square kilometres
(Enter)
(Enter)
(Enter)

Former Soviet Union	22.40(Enter)
Canada	9.98(Enter)
China	9.56(Enter)
United States	9.36(Enter)
EC (12 countries)	2.25(Enter)

(1) First type the heading: 'Area of each country ...'
(2) Then press Enter three times.
(3) Display the Tab Set dialog box by selecting *Tab Set* from the *Layout* menu.

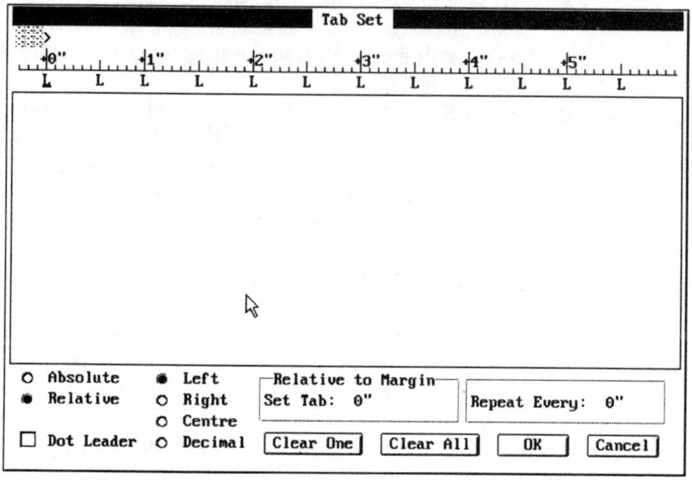

The current tab settings will now appear on the screen. The default setting is a tab stop every half inch beginning at the left, as can be seen by the capital L. Several buttons and options are displayed in the bottom part of the dialog window. Here is a brief outline of their functions:

Set Tab/ Repeat Every	When you have set a tab, the exact position of the tab is shown in this box.
Clear One	If you click on a tab on the ruler, you can subsequently delete it by clicking on this button.
Clear All	If you click on this button, all the stops on the ruler will be cleared.

The Absolute and Relative option buttons determine whether the tab stops are placed in relation to the left-hand edge of the paper (Absolute) or the left margin

(Relative). If you select the left margin as the reference point, the tab stops do not need to be respecified if you change the margin settings since the distance to the left margin always remains the same. This is the default setting.
The type of tab stop must also be specified:

Left	This is for left-aligned tabs. If a left-aligned tab is activated by pressing the Tab key, the text will shift to the right as normally. An L appears on the ruler.
Right	For right-aligned tabs. If this tab setting is activated, the text will shift leftwards when you press the Tab key. An R is shown on the ruler.
Centre	For centred tabs. If this tab setting is activated, the text you type is centred around this tab setting. A C appears on the ruler.
Decimal	For decimal tabs. We shall discuss this topic shortly. On the ruler a D is shown.
Dot Leader	You can add dots which will be shown up to each tab stop. This type of display is very useful for lists of contents for instance: Foreword .... 3 Chapter 1 .... 10 Chapter 2 .... 40 For example: you wish to install a right-aligned dot leader tab 5 inches from the left margin. Open the Tab Set dialog window by selecting that option from the *Layout* menu. Remove all tab stops by clicking on the Clear All button. Select the Right option button and activate the Dot Leader check box. Click on the Relative button and then on Set Tab. Type 5" here and confirm your specifications by clicking on OK. A right-

aligned tab is now installed. If you now activate this tab by pressing the Tab key, the space up to the next tab stop will be filled with dots.

(4) Back to our exercise. We opened the Tab Set dialog window in step 3. We do not wish to use the standard tab setting so we delete this by clicking on Clear All.
(5) We shall place a decimal tab 2.5 inches from the left margin. Activate the Decimal option and type 2.5" behind Set Tab. The Relative option button should be activated.
(6) Press Enter. It is possible to specify additional stops behind Set Tab, confirming each one by pressing Enter. However, we shall confine ourselves here to just the one tab stop.
(7) Exit the dialog window by clicking on the OK button.
(8) Type ‘Former Soviet Union’ and press the Tab key twice to create some space.
(9) Type the number 22.40 and press Enter.
(10) You can enter the names and the numbers for the other countries in the same way (see steps 8 and 9). You will see that the numbers around the align character, in this case the point, are centred. The message ‘Align char = .’ appears on the status line.
(11) Save this document using the *Save As* command from the *File* menu and call it TAB.

Notes

- It is also possible to install tabs using the mouse. To do this, choose the *Tab Set* option from the *Layout* menu and double click at the required position on the ruler.
- You can remove a default tab setting completely by removing the relevant code.
- Tab settings are valid from the current cursor position onwards.

- If you only wish to have the tab settings apply to one or more paragraphs, select the appropriate text before specifying the tab settings.
- You can alter the position of the tab stops on the ruler by opening the Tab Set dialog window by choosing the *Tab Set* option from the *Layout* menu. Then click on the tab stop on the ruler which you wish to alter. The cursor flashes under that position. You can now use the key combinations Ctrl-Cursor Right and Ctrl-Cursor Left to shift the tab stop to the right or left.

6.8 Superscript and subscript

With WordPerfect you can have individual characters or whole passages of text placed above or below the line. This makes it easier to write chemical and arithmetical formulas (H_2O; $a^2 + b^2 = c^2$).

In the previous section you saved a document under the name TAB. We want to alter the heading of this file slightly: instead of 'square kilometres' we are going to write 'km^2':

(1) If the TAB document is not on the screen, retrieve it by selecting *Open* from the *File* menu. Type TAB and click on OK.
(2) Delete the words 'square kilometres'.
(3) Type 'km2' in their place.
(4) The cursor is after the 2 you have just typed. Press Alt-F4 and Cursor Left. The number is now marked.
(5) Select the *Size/Position* option from the *Font* menu. Then select *Superscript* from the submenu.
(6) The number 2 is shown as required on the screen.

Note
If you mark the 2 again and then the *Normal* option from the *Font* menu, the number is displayed in normal size once more.

6.9 Justification

6.9.1 Justification on/off

A fully justified text has a straight left and right margin. In this book the text is fully justified. An alternative to left and right justification is a text with an irregular right margin. You have probably been typing with an irregular right margin up until now.

The default setting in WordPerfect is full justification, but you can give existing text an irregular right margin if you wish. We shall now begin a new document to practise this. (You may of course make use of your own texts or reopen the HOBBIT document instead.)

(1) Select *New* from the *File* menu.
(2) Type the text as shown or type your own text.

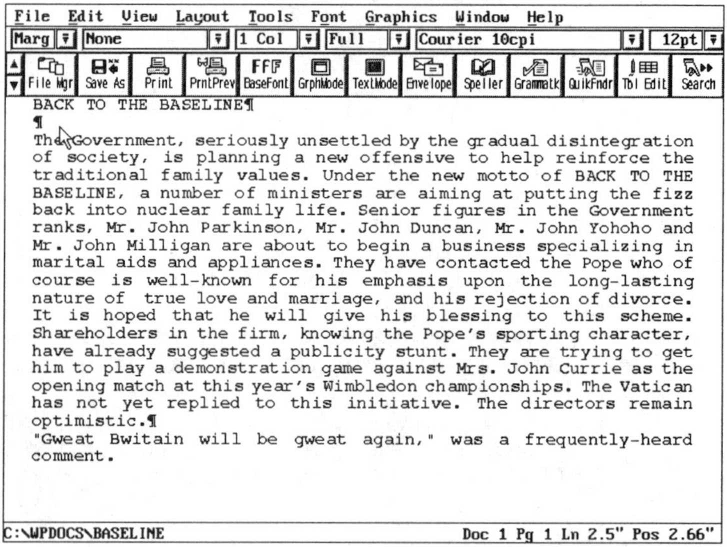

(3) Move the cursor to the beginning of the text
(4) Select *Justification* from the *Layout* menu. Click on *Left* in the subsequent submenu. The text acquires

a ragged right edge.

(5) Save the document under the name BASELINE.

Notes

- If you wish to align only a certain part of a text, mark that part first before selecting the *Justification* option from the *Layout* menu.
- Instead of selecting the command from the menu, you can simply double click on the required option on the ribbon. Click on the arrow next to *Full*. A list opens. Double click on *Left*.

6.9.2 Print preview

Although the document is shown on the screen in the graphics mode in much the same way as it will come out of the printer, it is advisable to use the *Print Preview* feature to perform a final check. If you activate this function, the text is shown exactly as it will be reproduced on the printer. It is not possible, however, to edit this text in this mode.

(1) With your text on the screen, select the *Print Preview* option from the *File* menu. The text disappears for a moment and then is displayed as it will come out of the printer. You cannot edit it, but if you have a lengthy text you can browse through the various pages (see section 2.2).

The Print Preview window is divided into four parts.

Menubar — The menubar with the available options is shown along the top of the window. The *File* menu only provides the *Setup* and *Close* (back to the document) commands. The *View* menu enables you to manipulate the display of the document in the Print Preview window. Sizing the display is the most important function here. The *Facing Pages*

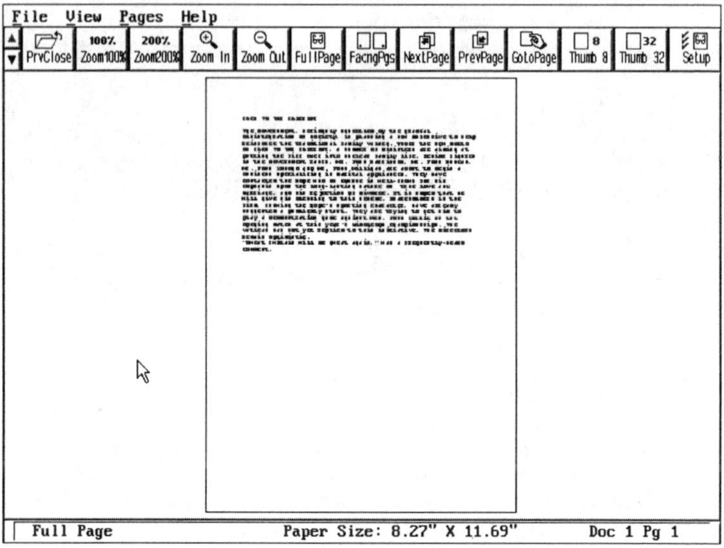

option displays two pages on the screen. The *Pages* menu provides options for displaying specific pages of the document.

Button bar — The button bar is displayed under the menu bar. The button bar enables you to select certain options provided in the menus quickly and easily using the mouse.

Document display — The largest area of the screen is reserved for the document itself. It is now displayed on the screen as it will come out of the printer.

Status bar — The type of display is shown on the left. If this is not the standard Full Page setting, the zoom percentage is indicated here. The current paper size is shown in the middle of this line and the document and page number at the right-hand side.

(2) Select *Close* from the *File* menu to return to the document.

6.10 Page format

6.10.1 Setting top and bottom margins

The *Margins* option from the *Layout* menu enables you to specify the settings for the top and bottom margins. Changing the number of lines to be left unused at the top and bottom also has consequences for the maximum number of lines that will fit on each page. The default top and bottom margins in WordPerfect are six lines (equivalent to 1" or 2.54 cm). Normally the top margin is not displayed on the screen. If you wish to check this, select *Print Preview* from the *File* menu or *Page Mode* from the *View* menu.

We shall now increase the top margin of our practice document:

(1) Load the BASELINE document if it is not still on the screen.
(2) If not already there, move the cursor to the beginning of the document via Home, Home, Cursor Up.
(3) Select the *Margins* option from the *Layout* menu.
(4) Click on the Top Margin box and type 4".
(5) Close the dialog box by clicking on OK.
(6) If you now examine the document using *Print Preview* from the *File* menu, you will see that the top margin has been considerably increased.

You can of course print the document on paper and compare it to a previous version on the screen to see the change in the margin.
We shall deal extensively with printing in the following chapter.

Note
Always give this command at the beginning of a page otherwise any changes to the top margin will only take effect on the following page. If the *Auto Code Placement* option is activated (*File* menu, *Setup, Environment*), the code will be placed at the beginning of the page regardless of the current position in the text.

6.10.2 Page numbering

Page numbering is especially useful in long documents when you need to locate certain passages. If you wish to have the pages automatically numbered in succession, select the *Page* option from the *Layout* menu. It is also possible to integrate the page numbers in the headers and footers (see further section 9.2).

Here we shall be dealing with the first of these options. We want to put a page number in the middle at the bottom of every page.

(1) Load the BASELINE document if necessary.
(2) Since the page numbering feature also takes effect from the current cursor position, move the cursor to the beginning of the document via Home, Home, Cursor Up.
(3) Select *Page* from the *Layout* menu and then click on Page Numbering. The following dialog window appears:

Page Number Position	This option enables you to determine where the page number is to be printed on the paper. None is the default setting here. Click on this option and you will be able to choose from a list provided. Click on an option and then on OK. You will return to the Page Numbering dialog box.
Page Number	This option enables you select the first number be placed in your docu-

ment and to specify the style of the number applied: normal numbers or Roman numbers.

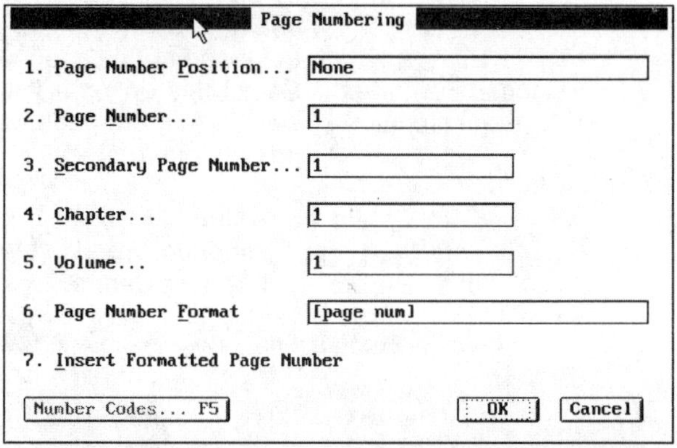

Secondary Page Number
: This option enables you to apply a second set of numbers to a page. These work just like page numbers. Both page numbers and secondary page numbers increase automatically.

Chapter/Volume
: These options can be very convenient when you have a lengthy document with various sections. Each page can be numbered according to its place in the document and can also have its own number which refers to its position in the section. Always move the cursor to the beginning of the page when specifying page numbers.

Page Number Format
: This option determines how the page number is displayed. The default setting, [page num], which cannot be deleted, will display only the page number when page numbering is activated. But you can add extra text if you wish such as 'This is page - '. The screen then shows:

This is page - [page num], where the code is replaced by the appropriate page number. You can specify any text of your choice (max. 48 characters) in front of and behind the [page num] code.

Insert Formatted Page Number — Select this option if you want to insert the current page number at the present cursor position.

(4) Click on the Page Number Position option to activate the page numbering. Specify the position, in this case we want Bottom Centre.

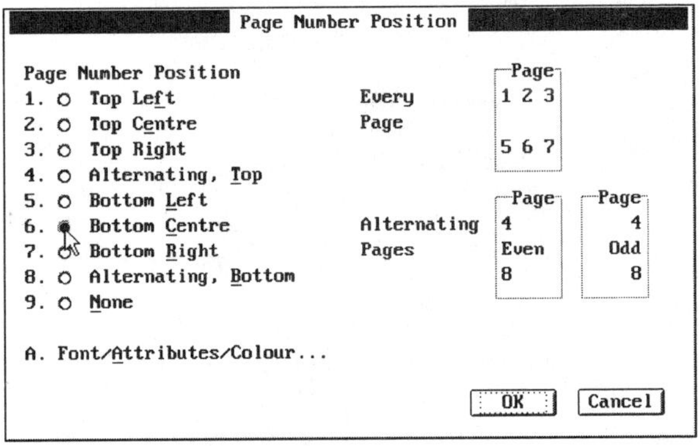

(5) Click on OK to confirm your specifications.

The result of your efforts will only become apparent when you have printed the document or have made use of the Print Preview function. On the normal screen, you only know that page numbering is on by the code (Page Num Pos with a position indication) when you press the Reveal Codes key (F11).

6.10.3 Hard page break

When you are working with WordPerfect you do not need to worry about dividing the document up into pages. As soon as you reach the end of a page, WordPerfect automatically switches over to the next page. The changeover to the next page is indicated by a dotted line running across the screen.

You can adjust the number of lines that fit on a page via the *Margins* option from the *Layout* menu. But you can also make a new page manually. Move the cursor to where you want to start a new page. Select the *Alignment* option from the *Layout* menu and then select *Hard Page* from the submenu. An easier method of creating a hard page break is simply to press Ctrl-Enter. A double dotted line will appear on the screen to show that a hard page break has been inserted. You can cancel this new page by deleting the code that goes with it ([HPg]).

6.10.4 Setting paper size

The number of lines that fit on a page is determined initially by the size of the paper you are using. The default size is A4. But you can also set WordPerfect to any size of paper you want. The available formats depend on the capabilities of the printer installed.

By way of illustration we want to go through the steps for selecting A4 Landscape for the HP DeskJet printer. This means that the document will be printed lengthways on the paper. You load WordPerfect and you have a clear screen. Now proceed as follows:

(1) Move the cursor to the beginning of the page where you want the new size to apply.
(2) Select the *Page* option from the *Layout* menu. The click on the *Paper Size/Type* option (nr.4). The dialog window shown overleaf appears on the screen.

We shall first examine the lower part of this window:

Orientation — The paper will be printed in the normal vertical way (portrait) or hori-

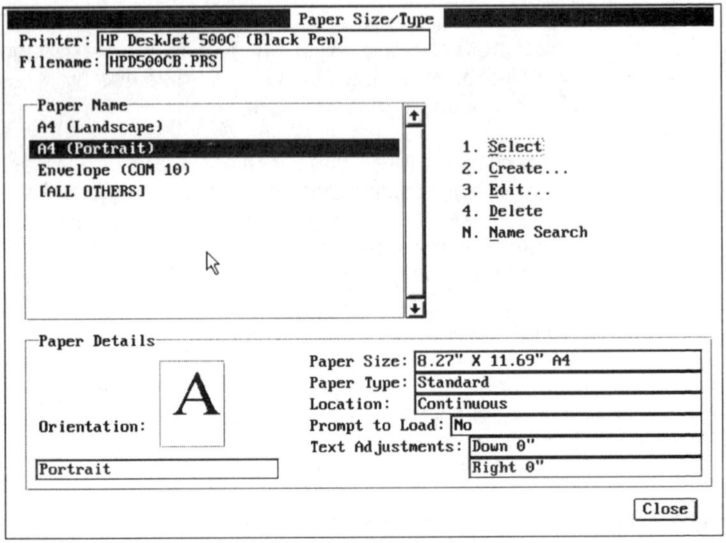

zontally (landscape). If you click on A4 Landscape in the Paper Name section, the orientation here will be altered.

Paper Size — This is the currently valid paper format.

Paper Type — The default setting is Standard. Select Envelope or ALL OTHERS from the section above if you wish to specify other settings here.

Location — This option deals with the way in which the paper is loaded in the printer. Click on Select, Create or Edit to change these settings (for Manual or Sheet Feeder).

Prompt to Load — If No is shown here, the text will be printed immediately the print command is given. If Yes is shown here, printing will only start after confirmation is given via the *Control Printer* option (*File* menu, *Print/ Fax*). This can be useful when the

	paper has to be manually fed into the printer.
Text Adjustments	You can specify here the position where the text is to be printed on the paper without altering the document margins.

The currently active setting is shown inversely in the upper part of the window. If the specifications shown here do not correspond to those of your computer, click on a paper format in the list and then click on Edit to make alterations to the standard settings.

(3) Select the A4 (Landscape) option by clicking on it and then confirm this choice by clicking on Select.

WordPerfect automatically adjusts the margins and the number of lines per page to the new paper format.

By removing the code, you can return to the previous paper format settings.

The Create option in the Paper Size/Type dialog box enables you to define a paper format which is not provided in the list.

Exercises

(1) Complete the following: To underline a passage of existing text this text must first be __________. Then you can activate underlining by pressing the key combination _____-_____.

(2) You want to remove the underlining under the word WordPerfect. Complete the following: First move the ________ to the ________ of the word from which you want to remove the underlining. Then activate the _____________ feature using the key combination _____-_____. Now move the cursor to the right of the ______ which represents the Underline function. You can now delete this ______ using the _________ key.

(3) How do you activate the Centre function?

____

(4) You want the left margin of an entire document to begin at position 2". How do you do this?

____

____

(5) WordPerfect suggests hyphenating a word in a particular place. Which button do you press to confirm this suggestion?

____

(6) How do you set hyphenation with your assistance? Write down which keys you press:

____

____

(7) Complete the following: By pressing the Indent key (_____) you can indent a paragraph in WordPerfect to the next __________.

(8) You want to put a right-aligned tab with a dot leader at position 5". Write down which commands and keys you have to use:

____

(9) In WordPerfect you cannot always see the text as it will subsequently be printed. How can you display the text on the screen in this way?

____

(10) You have a document three pages long and you want to set the line spacing to one-and-a-half from page 2 onwards. Write down the steps in this process:

____

____

Answers

(1) To underline a passage of existing text this text must first be *highlighted*. Then you can activate underlining by pressing *Ctrl-U* or *F8*.

(2) First move the *cursor* to the *beginning* of the word from which you want to remove the underlining. Then activate the *Reveal Codes* feature using the key combination *Alt-F3*. Now move the cursor to the right of the *code* which represents the Underline function. You can now delete this *code* using the *Backspace* key.

(3) By means of the *Alignment* option in the *Layout* menu. Select *Centre* from the submenu. You can also simply press *Shift-F6*

(4) Move the cursor to the beginning of the text. Select *Margins* from the *Layout* menu. Type 2" in the *Left Margin* box. Click on *OK* to confirm the setting.

(5) The *Insert Hyphen* button.

(6) *Ctrl-hyphen.*

(7) *F4;*
to the next *tab stop*

(8) Select *Tab Set* from the *Layout* menu. Activate the *Dot Leader* and *Right* options. Type 5" behind *Set Tab*. Confirm by pressing Enter. Ensure that *Relative* is activated. Close the dialog window by clicking on *OK*.

(9) Select the *Print Preview* option from the *File* menu.

(10) Place the cursor at the beginning of page 2. Select the *Line* option from the *Layout* menu and click on the *Line Spacing* option. Type 1.5 in the corresponding text box. Confirm the setting by clicking on *OK*.

7 Printing

In this chapter we shall be looking at the options for printing text and the layout of texts to be printed. The choice of font is an important aspect of the document layout at this stage.

7.1 Printing blocks of text, a page, the whole document

With WordPerfect you can print individual pages, blocks of text or whole documents. We are going to take a closer look at some of these features. Load the practice document HOBBIT. First we are going to print a **block of text**. To do this we use the Block feature:

(1) Make sure the printer is ready to print (see section 2.8).
(2) Move the cursor to the T of 'They walked in single file'.
(3) Switch on the Block feature by pressing F12.
(4) Press Enter. You have now highlighted a paragraph.
(5) Select the *Print/Fax* option from the *File* menu.

The Blocked Text option is activated in the Print section.

(6) Click on the Print Button to start the print procedure.

You know from chapter 2 that you can print a whole document by means of the *Print/Fax* option from the *File* menu. If you wish to only print one page of your document, select the Page option in the Print/Fax dialog window. Proceed as follows:

(1) Load the document.
(2) Move the cursor to the page you want to print. You

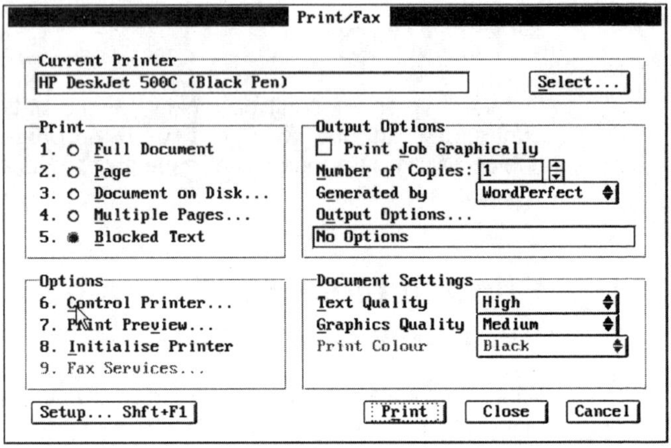

can send the cursor straight to the relevant page by selecting the *Go to* option from the *Edit* menu.

(3) Then select the *Print/Fax* option from the *File* menu. Click on the Page button in the Print section.

Note

You can choose the Multiple Pages option in the Print/Fax dialog window if you want to print various pages from the open file. If you click on this option, the following dialog window appears:

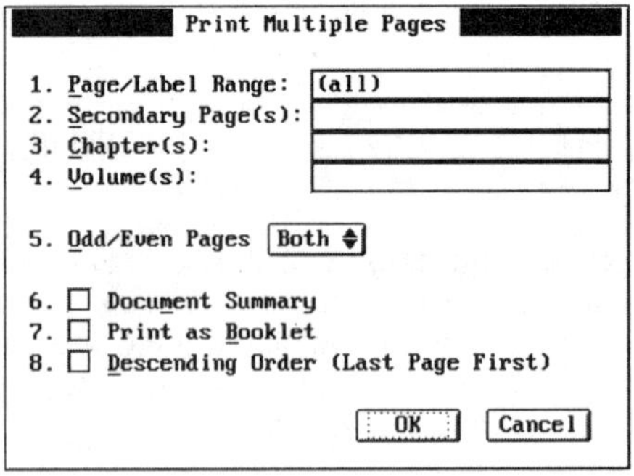

Specify in the Page/Label Range which pages are to be printed. The following section outlines these options further.

7.2 Printing documents from disk

If the document called HOBBIT is still on the screen, you can save it using the *Save* option from the *File* menu.
In WordPerfect you can also print files which are not displayed on the screen but which you have on your harddisk or floppy. We shall assume that the file with the name HOBBIT is stored on the harddisk in the WPDOCS directory.

(1) Select *Print/Fax* from the *File* menu.
(2) Select the Document on Disk option (nr.3) from the Print section. The following dialog box appears:

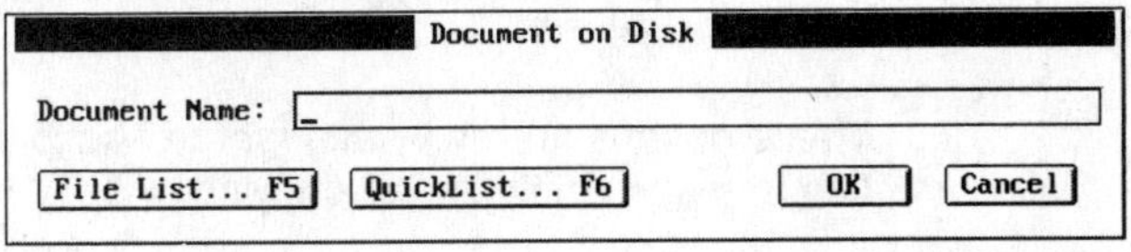

(3) Type the name of your text in the Document on Disk box: **c:\wpdocs\hobbit** and press Enter. If you do not know the exact name of the directory and file, click on the File List button and confirm the subsequent display by clicking on OK. A dialog box appears showing a list of files from which you can choose. When you have done so, click on Select to confirm your choice. The Print Multiple Pages dialog window appears.

Specify the part(s) of the text to be printed in the Page/Label Range box. The default setting, (all), means that the entire document will be printed. Now specify the parts of the document you want printed.

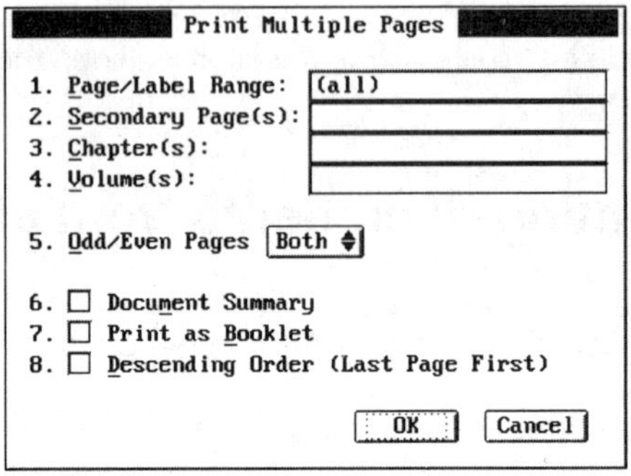

type	**effect**
3-	print from page 3 to the end of the document
7-10	print from page 7 to page 10
3,5,7	print pages 3, 5 and 7
3,7-10	print page 3 and pages 7 to 10
-7	print from the beginning of the document to page 7

These options are only valid for the Multiple Pages option from the Print/Fax dialog window.

(4) Since our document only consists of one page, you can confirm the print instruction by clicking on OK. WordPerfect will then print the whole document.

Notes

- Section 2.7 tells you what you can do if the print job is not executed. If necessary, check that the printer settings are correct.
- The Multiple Pages dialog box provides the possibility of printing all pages from a particular section or only the even or odd pages of the selected section. If you click on the Descending Order option, the pages will be printed in reverse order of sequence.
- If further problems occur when printing, select the Control Printer option in the Print/Fax window. The

corresponding window displays the current print jobs and any error messages if present. Rectify the problem, by putting paper in the printer for instance, or switching the printer to Online. Set the printing process in motion by clicking on the Go button.

7.3 The Control Printer function

The Control Printer function allows you to exercise control over the printing of one or more documents. To display this feature press Shift-F7, 6 or select *File, Print/Fax, Control Printer*. The following dialog box appears:

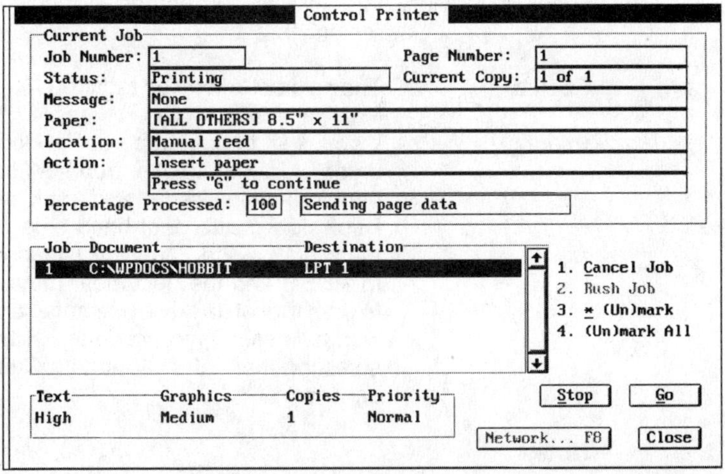

This window can be divided into three areas:

- The area at the top contains instructions regarding the document currently being printed (the current print job). If the printer is not functioning, an indication of the problem will be given behind Action.
- Below it is a list of print jobs.
- At the very bottom is a menu you use to control the print jobs.

The specification of a number of lines to be printed is called a print job. In WordPerfect you can send several print jobs to the printer at the same time. These jobs will be numbered and will be displayed in the Job List. They will be printed consecutively. The maximum number of print jobs displayed in the Job List is three. You can, however, send more than three jobs to the printer.

Explanation of the menu at the bottom of the screen:

Text High	This indicates that the text will be printed in high resolution definition (good quality letters).
Graphics Medium	Graphics will be printed in medium resolution.
Copies	The number of copies required.
Priority	If you wish to have a particular document brought to the front of the print queue, select it and click on Rush Job at the right-hand side of the window. The Priority will change to RUSH and the document moved to the top of the list. Remove unwanted documents from the list by selecting them and clicking on Cancel Job.

Notes

- Cancel Job completely cancels the current print job, the job you have highlighted or the job(s) you have marked with an asterisk. If you cancel a job and then decide to print it after all, you must send it to the printer again by means of the *Print/Fax* command from the *File* menu.
- Stop temporarily stops the current print job. If you stop a job, you can either restart it or cancel it.
- If a print job has already been sent to the printer, WordPerfect may not be able to stop it or cancel it

immediately. After cancelling it, you may have to reset the printer by switching it off then on again.

7.4 Other print features

Apart from the options described in the previous section, there are some other interesting ones in the Print/Fax dialog box. We shall mention the most important of these.

Output options

Print Job Graphically	Activate this option if the document is not printed as shown by the *Print Preview* option from the *File* menu.
Number of Copies	Type the required number of copies here.

Document Settings

Text Quality	This determines the quality of the printed text.
Graphics Quality	This determines the print quality of the images.

If you click on one of these options, a list opens showing the following possibilities: *Do Not Print, Draft, Medium, High*. Normally, the higher the quality, the longer the printer will take to produce the document. The first option in the list, Do Not Print, may come as a surprise. However, if you realize that you can combine images and text in one document, you can select this open to suppress either the text or the images in a document if required.

Options

Control Printer	This enables you to examine the printing situation, rectify print problems and determine print priority.
Print Preview	This option shows the document as it will come out of the printer.

7.5 Changing font

If you select the *Font* option from the *Font* menu, a dialog box appears in which you can choose various font options. Some of these options can also be specified by means of other commands in this menu (such as Bold and Underline).

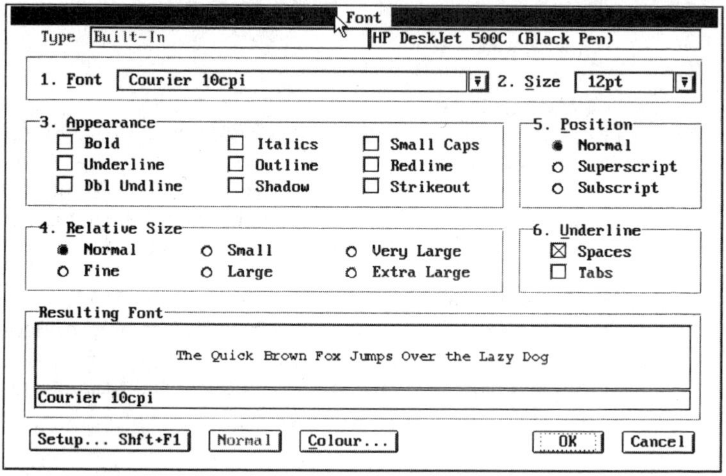

The first box, Font, enables you to select one of a number of fonts. The currently active font is indicated here. Click on this box. A list appears. The currently active font is shown in the list with an asterisk in front of its name. The number of fonts available depends on the installed printer.

The Size text box enables you to set the font size. The unit of measurement here is points. There are 72 points to an inch (approx. 30 to one cm.)

The Appearance section enables you to determine the appearance of the letters themselves (Bold, Underline etc.).

The Relative Size enables you to specify the size of a letter in relation to the normal size of the chosen font.

The Position options determine the position of characters in relation to the other characters.

Notes

- If you set these options while you are typing, you can switch them off again by selecting the same option from the *Font* menu. If you wish to apply them to an existing text, select the required passages first.
- If you choose a certain font or font size without first selecting a section of text, the chosen font or font size comes into force at the cursor position. The previous font is deactivated but existing text retains the previous font and size. If you select a new font unintentionally, place the cursor at the position where you gave the command and press Alt-F3. You can then locate and delete the code.
- It is also possible to select a new font or font size from the ribbon.

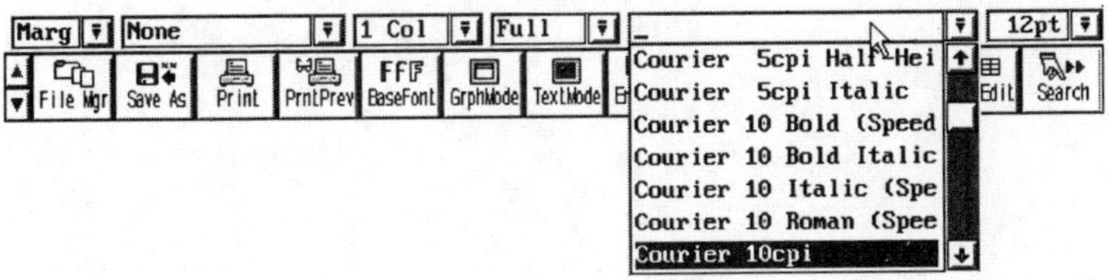

- Alterations to the font are shown in the Resulting Font example box in the Font dialog box.
- When using Footnotes and Endnotes (see also chapter 9), a small problem may arise. If you have chosen a different font via the *Font* option from the *Font* menu and you then create footnotes, the footnotes may be printed in a different font than the one used for the normal text. Normally, footnotes are printed using a default font. However, you can alter this default setting by selecting *Document* from the *Layout* menu. Then choose Initial Font. If

you select this option, not only the text but also the footnotes and the endnotes etc. will be printed in the chosen font.

Exercises

(1) On the TEXT directory on the harddisk (drive C:) there is a file 20 pages long with the name EXERCISE. You want to print pages 10 and 12 and pages 15 to 19 of this file. Write down the commands and keys you would use:

____

____

(2) You want an additional copy printed of each printed document. Write down which commands and keys you would use.

____

(3) Complete the following: If you want to display existing text in italics, you must first ________ the passage in question. Then open the __________ dialog window by selecting this option from the __________ menu. Finally select __________ by clicking on the appropriate check box.

(4) Complete the following: If you want to change the font of existing text, first move the __________ to where you want the different font to begin. Then select the __________ option from the _________ menu. A new font can be chosen in the dialog box. This new font will remain effective until the _________ of the document unless you specify a different font further on in the text by choosing _________ from the _________ menu.

Answers

(1) Select the *Print/Fax* command from the *File* menu. Click on Document on Disk. Type the name c:\text\exercise in the Document Name box. Confirm using OK. Type 10,12,15-19 in the Page/Label Range box. Click on OK and Print.

(2) Select *Print/Fax* from the *File* menu. Type 2 in the Number of Copies box.

(3) If you want to display existing text in italics, you must first *mark* the passage in question. Then open the *Font* dialog window by selecting this option from the *Font* menu. Finally select *Italics* by clicking on the appropriate check box.

(4) If you want to change the font of existing text, first move the *cursor* to where you want the different font to begin. Then select the *Font* option from the *Font* menu. A new font can be chosen in the dialog box. This new font will remain effective until the *end* of the document, unless you specify a different font further on in the text by choosing *Font* from the *Font* menu.

8 File management

In this chapter we shall be taking a closer look at the management of files. Part of the management of files and disks takes place at DOS level. In this section you will become familiar with the functions of the File Manager. The File Manager enables you to implement a large number of tasks for which you would otherwise require complicated commands in the operating system.

8.1 The list of files

The File Manager enables you to display a list of all the files stored on harddisk or floppy. Proceed as follows:

(1) Select the *File Manager* option from the *File* menu.
(2) Type, in the Directory text box, the name of the directory containing the files you wish to examine. Imagine that you wish to look at the files in the C:\WPDOCS directory. Type C:\WPDOCS*.* in this box if it is not already shown there. The asterisks *.* mean that all files in this directory are to be shown. But if there are many files in a directory, it may be advisable to make use of the facility of only displaying a certain amount of the files. To do this, you can apply the MS-DOS wildcards, the asterisk and the question mark (* and ?). For example, if you type *.TXT, only those files with the extension TXT will be shown. Files which begin with a W can be displayed by typing W*.*.

Then click on OK or press Enter. A dialog window appears.

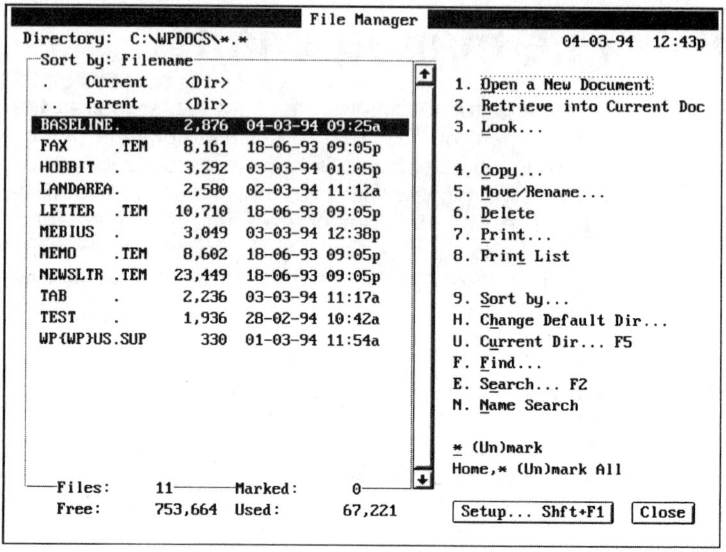

Directory: C:\WPDOCS*.* The currently active directory is shown at the top of the dialog box. The asterisks indicate that all files in the list are shown. Note that it is advisable to make use of directories to classify your files. If you have created lots of files it can be useful to divide them into categories so that you know where to find them. You could compare this to a supermarket for instance where goods are ordered according to type instead of being thrown on a heap. You can divide directories into subdirectories to store the various files, one subdirectory for letters, one for reports, one for finance etc.

Sort by: Filename The left part of this section shows the files in the currently active directory in alphabetical order. The word 'Parent' is shown at the top of this list. This indicates that there is a higher directory, in other words, the current directory is a subdirectory of this parent directory. In our example, that is the root directory on the harddisk, C:\. If you double click on Parent you will switch to that directory where you will see all the directories stored in the root directory. Double click on WPDOCS <Dir> to switch back to the directory where we were working.

The date and time are also displayed at the top right-hand corner of the window. The bottom part of the window shows the number of files contained in the directory, the number of marked files, the available disk capacity and the amount of disk space currently occupied.

8.2 Marking, opening, deleting, renaming and copying files

You can perform a great number of tasks by using the File Manager. The relevant files must first be marked. This is done by clicking on the file name using the mouse. If you wish to select several files in one go, hold down the Shift key while doing this. An asterisk appears in front of the corresponding file. If you wish to remove the marking, click on the file name once more while holding down the Shift key. The asterisk disappears.

When you have marked a file, click on the first option in the command list at the right of the window, Open a New Document. You can now edit the document.
It is also possible to delete a marked file. For example, we shall delete the TAB document which we created earlier and no longer need.

(1) Click on the TAB file in the list.
(2) Click on Delete. A question appears on the screen:

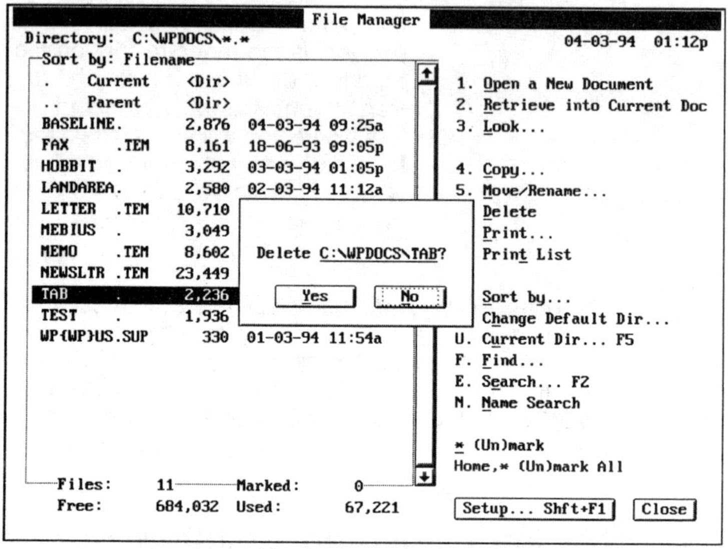

(3) This is a safeguard question. Click on Yes.
(4) Click on Close to conclude working with the File Manager.

It is also possible to rename files. We shall allocate a new name to the HOBBIT file.

(1) Select the *File Manager* option from the *File* menu and confirm the C:\WPDOCS*.* directory by pressing Enter.
(2) Click on the name HOBBIT.
(3) Click on the Move/Rename command.
(4) Type the new name BILBO and click on OK.

The name HOBBIT disappears and is replaced by BILBO.

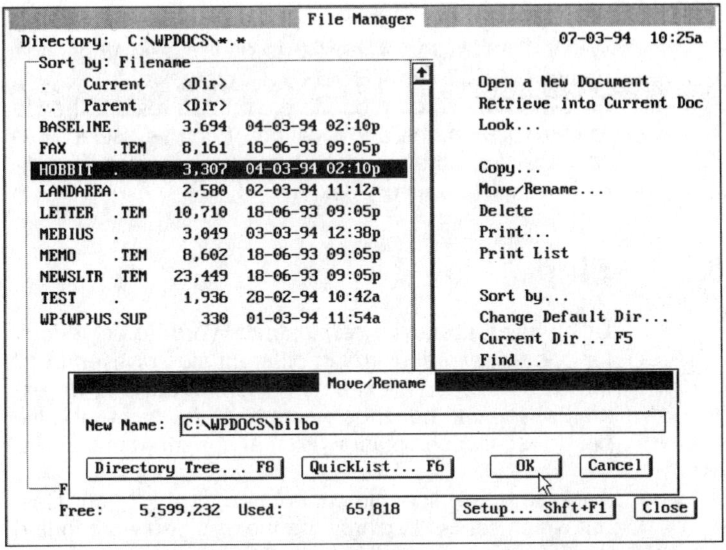

If you wish to copy a file, proceed in the same way, but of course you have to choose Copy instead of Move/Rename. Then specify the destination for the file, for instance A: if you want to copy the file to the diskette in drive A:.

Note

The Move/Rename function provides an additional possibility. You can move a file to a different drive and/or directory. We shall give a hypothetical example which you cannot use here with these files but which you can use for your own text files. Imagine you wish to move the BILBO file to an existing different directory (e.g. BOOKS) under a different name (e.g. FOREST).

(1) Select the *File Manager* option from the *File* menu. Press Enter to confirm the current directory C:\WPDOCS.
(2) Click on the name BILBO and select the Move/Rename option.
(3) Type the entire new name in the text box: C:\BOOKS\FOREST.
(4) Click on OK.

The BILBO file name then disappears from the WPDOCS directory. The file is now stored under the name FOREST in the BOOKS directory.
Following the same procedure, you can restore the file to its original name and location of course. Select *File Manager* from the *File* menu and type the required directory in the Directory box.

8.3 Find

Using this feature you can instruct WordPerfect to look for one or several words in different files or even in all the files. This is an extremely useful feature if, for example, you can no longer remember the name of a file but do recall a particular word that appeared in that file.

An example (which you cannot carry out with our files, but which serves to clarify the theory): you want to find the files in which the word 'want' appears:

(1) Select *File Manager* from the *File* menu and confirm the directory by pressing Enter.
(2) Click on the Find... option. The following dialog box appears.

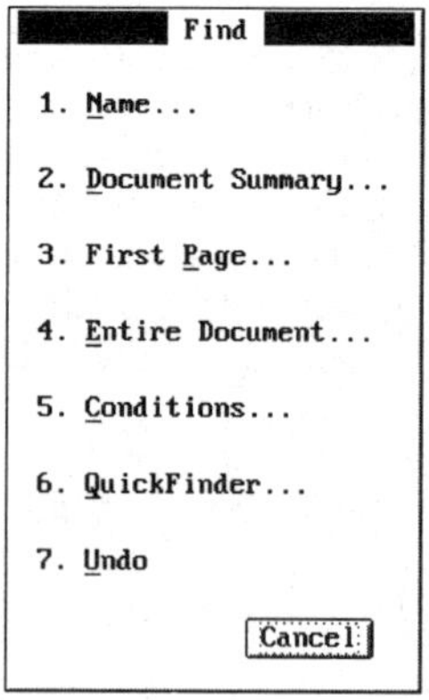

(3) Select the Entire Document option so that the complete text of the files displayed will be examined.
(4) Type the word 'want' in the Word Pattern text box.

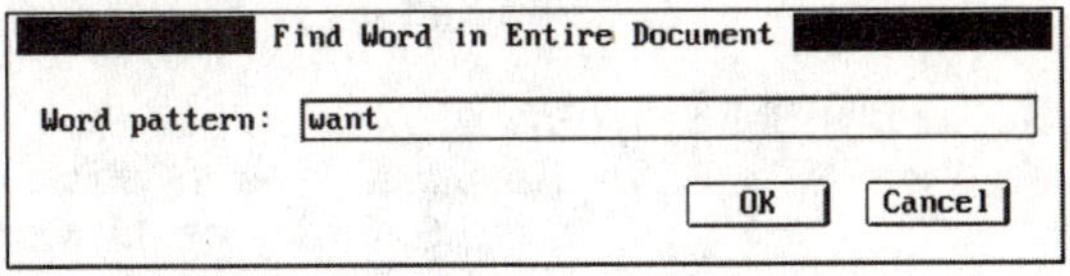

(5) Start the procedure by clicking on OK.
(6) All files containing the specified word will be displayed in a window at the end of the search process. You can click on the file names and employ the Look option to examine that file. When you have found the file you were looking for, mark it and select the first option Open a New Document to open the file.

Notes

- If the search fails to find the word, the status line will display the message 'Not Found'. In this case check that you have spelled the word you want correctly.
- When you enter a search pattern, you can use asterisks and question marks as wildcards. Some examples:

sl?p	Result: all files in which words such as slap, slip and slop appear are marked.
s*shine	Result: all files in which words such as sunshine, shoeshine, etc., appear are marked.

- When you enter a search pattern (step 5), you can also use logical operators, such as the semicolon and the space (for AND) and the comma (for OR). Some examples:

Sunday(space)Saturday(Enter)
or
Sunday;Saturday(Enter)

Result: all files in which both words (Saturday **and** Sunday) appear are marked.

Sunday,Saturday(Enter)

Result: all files in which **either** the word Saturday **or** the word Sunday appears are marked.

8.4 Switching drives

Of course, you can switch drives when working with WordPerfect. We now wish to display the files stored on a diskette in drive A:.

(1) Insert the diskette into drive A:.
(2) Select the *File Manager* option from the *File* menu.
(3) Click on the Directory Tree button or press F8.

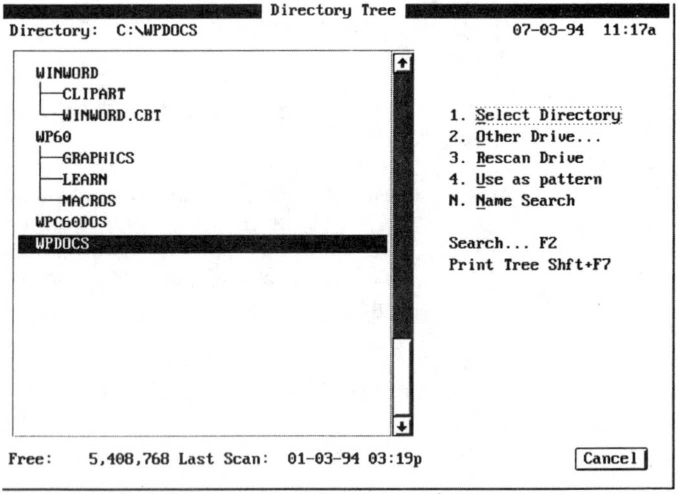

The left-hand part of the window displays a hierarchical structure of directory names. The right-hand section shows a number of commands.

(4) Select the Other Drive command.
(5) A window showing the available drives appears.
(6) Click on the required drive, A: and then on Select.

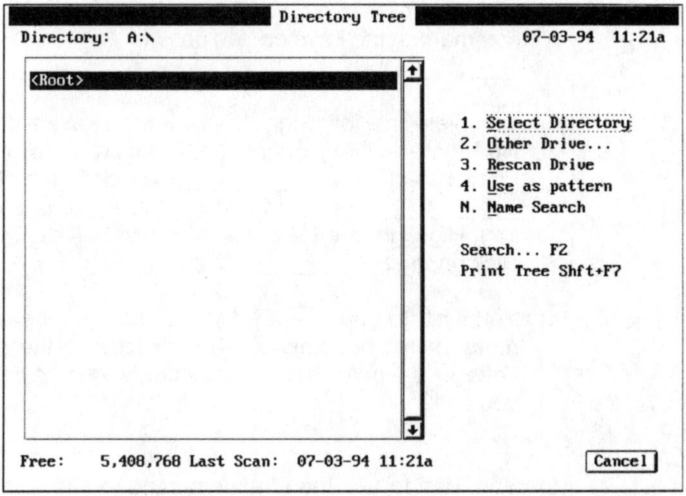

(7) The statement Directory: A:\ is shown at the top of the window, indicating that the switch has indeed taken place correctly. Since there are no subdirectories in the root directory of the diskette, only the <Root> directory is shown here. Each formatted diskette has this.
(8) Click on the Select Directory option to display the contents of the diskette.

Exercises

(1) You want to see all the files in the default directory that begin with the letter K and have the extension .TXT. Which commands and keys do you use?

____

(2) You are in drive C: (harddisk) and you want to look at the list of files on the diskette in drive A:. Which commands and keys do you use?

____

(3) Complete the following: If you want to examine a file before actually opening it, proceed as follows. First select the __________ option from the __________ menu and specify the required directory. Highlight the file name in the list of files. Then click on the __________ option.

(4) You wish to copy the EXAMPLE file from the currently active directory on the harddisk to the diskette in drive A:. Which commands and keys do you use?

(5) You wish to use the Find command to find all files in which either the word 'Holland' or the word 'Netherlands' appears along with the words 'social structure'. Which commands or keys do you use?

____

Answers

(1) Select *File Manager* from the *File* menu. Type K*.TXT in the Directory box. Click on OK.

(2) Select *File Manager* from the *File* menu. Click on the Directory Tree button. Click on Other Drive, highlight drive A: and click on the Select button or press Enter.

(3) If you want to examine a file before actually opening it, proceed as follows. First select the *File Manager* option from the *File* menu and specify the required directory. Highlight the file name in the list of files. Then click on the Look option.

(4) Select *File Manager* from the *File* menu. Specify the required directory. Mark the EXAMPLE file in the file list. Select the Copy option. Type A: in the Copy Highlighted File To box. Press Enter.

(5) Select *File Manager* from the *File* menu. Specify the required directory. Select the Find option and then Entire Document. Type in the Word Pattern box: Holland,Netherlands;social structure. Click on OK.

9 Other word processing features

In this chapter you will be learning something about the use of the Search and Replace features, about creating endnotes and footnotes and about the Style feature, which is a quick and easy way to give your documents a different appearance.

9.1 Search and replace

9.1.1 Searching for words and codes

In contrast to the *Find* option from the *File Manager* in the *File* menu, the *Search* feature from the *Edit* menu applies only to the file on the screen at the time of the search. You can search both forwards and backwards. This feature is very important in WordPerfect because it enables you to search not only for words or passages of text but also codes.

Searching for words
We are going to look for the word 'led' in our practice document, which is now stored under the name BILBO.

(1) Load the document.
(2) Move the cursor to the beginning of the text.
(3) Select *Search* from the *Edit* menu. The following dialog window appears.

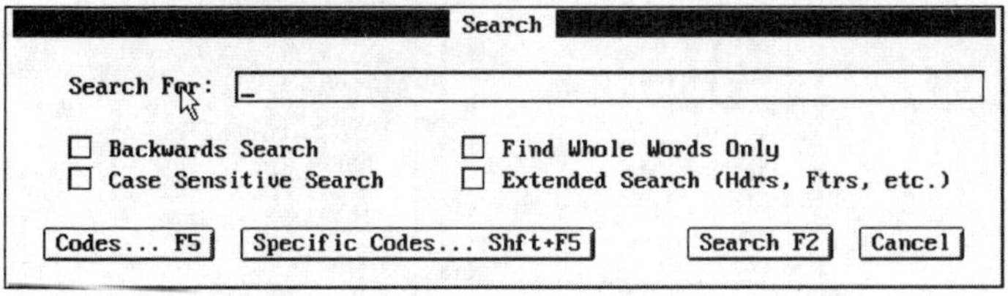

(4) Normally WordPerfect searches from the cursor onwards to the end of the text. If you wish to search backwards, place a cross in the appropriate box.
(5) Type the word *led* in the Search For box. If you type the word in small letters, the word will be found in the forms LED, Led and led. In addition, WordPerfect will also find the words, 'strangled', '-tangled', 'piled' etc. If you wish to search for the word *led* on its own, place a cross in the Find Whole Words Only box by clicking on it.
(6) Click on the Search F2 button, or press F2, to start the search.
(7) The cursor jumps to the position where the word first occurs. If you are not looking for this particular occurrence, repeat the search by pressing F2, F2.

Searching for codes

You can also locate any particular codes which are produced by keystrokes. The search procedure is then as follows:

(1) Move the cursor to the beginning of the document.
(2) Select *Search* from the *Edit* menu. Click on the Specific Codes button to display a list of codes. The following dialog window appears:

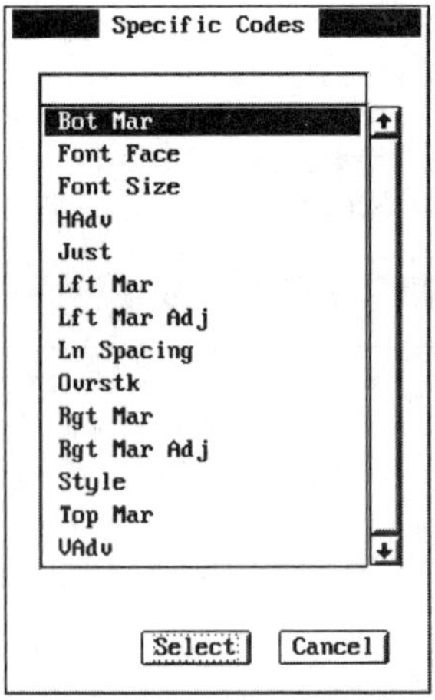

(3) Select the required code in the window by clicking on it. Click on the Select button to place the code in the Search For box.

In section 6.3, we centred the last line in our practice text. If this is no longer the case in your text, do that first. We wish to check this by means of the *Search* function.

(1) Since the title is centred as well, move the cursor to the first letter of the first paragraph.
(2) Select *Search* from the *Edit* menu.
(3) Click on the Specific Codes button. Mark the Just code in the list and then click on Select. In the subsequent dialog box, click on the Centre option button and confirm this by pressing Enter or clicking on OK. The screen now looks like this:

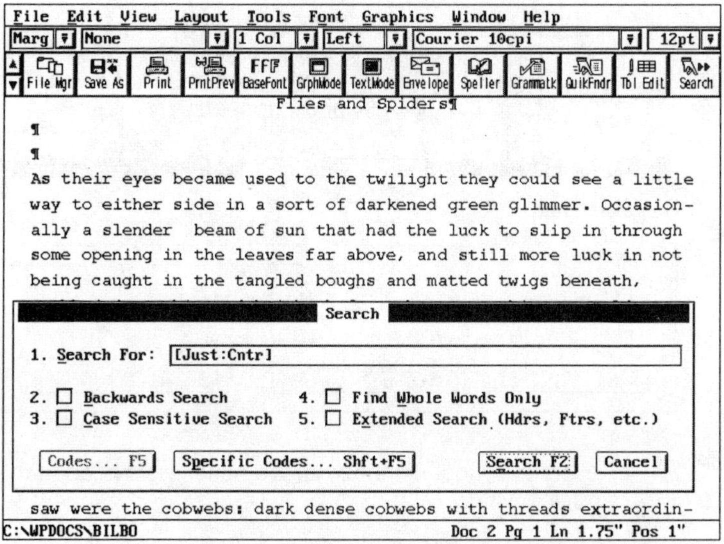

(4) Activate the search by clicking on the Search button or by pressing F2.
(5) The cursor appears behind the required code, in front of the text. You can check this by activating the Reveal Codes screen (F11).

Notes

- Normally the entire text is examined. If you also wish to have the footnotes, headers and footers, comments etc. examined, activate the Extended Search option on the Search dialog window.
- A maximum of 80 characters can be specified in the Search box.

9.1.2 Searching for, and replacing, (sections of) text

You can also search for and replace words, passages of text and codes. In our practice document (stored under the name BILBO) we want to replace the word '-path' with 'track':

(1) Load the document if necessary.
(2) Move the cursor to the beginning of the file.
(3) Select the *Replace* option from the *Edit* menu. The following dialog window appears:

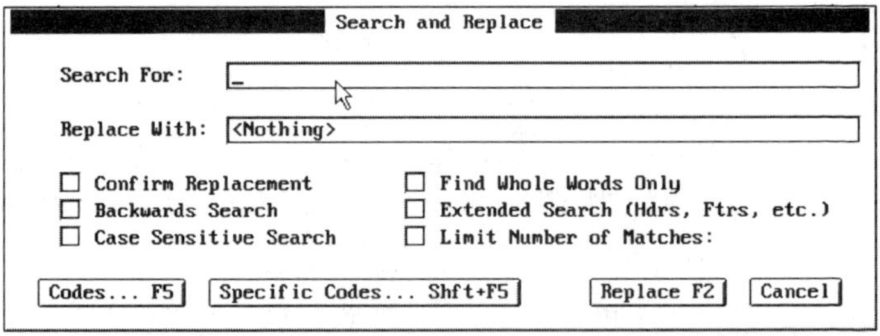

Here is a brief summary of the options provided in this dialog window:

Search For	Specify the text to be sought.
Replace With	The text which is to replace the sought text.
Confirm Replacement	If you confirm this option and set the procedure in motion, the following possibilities are provided:

Yes	The specified text is replaced.
No	The specified text is not replaced.
Replace All	All occurrences of the specified text are replaced.

(4)	Type *path* in the Search For box.
(5)	Type the word *track* in the Replace With box.
(6)	Press F2 to start Search and Replace.

You will see that the word we want is replaced four times. If it should appear in the document with a capital letter (which is not the case here), then WordPerfect will also write the replacement word with a capital letter. And since we did not use spaces when typing either the search string or the replacement text, WordPerfect would also replace the word ' footpath' - assuming that it appeared in the document - with 'foottrack'.

Note
If you select a section of text before activating the Search and Replace function, the search will be confined to the specified passage.

9.2 Creating headers and footers

A header is a line at the top of the page, a footer a line at the bottom. Headers and footers are lines which appear on every page in the same or slightly amended form. Look at almost any book, for example, and you will find a header or a footer showing the page number and often the title of the book and the current chapter as well.

In WordPerfect you can define two headers and two footers (A and B) for each page. Each header or footer in its turn can consist of several lines.

Although this feature is really only used for documents consisting of several pages, we are going to create a header and a footer for our practice document to give you an idea of how the feature works. We can incorporate page numbering in the header at the same time:

(1) Load the practice document (the document originally called HOBBIT and now stored as BILBO) if required.
(2) Move the cursor to the beginning of the page.
(3) Select the *Header/Footer/Watermark* option from the *Layout* menu. The following dialog window appears:

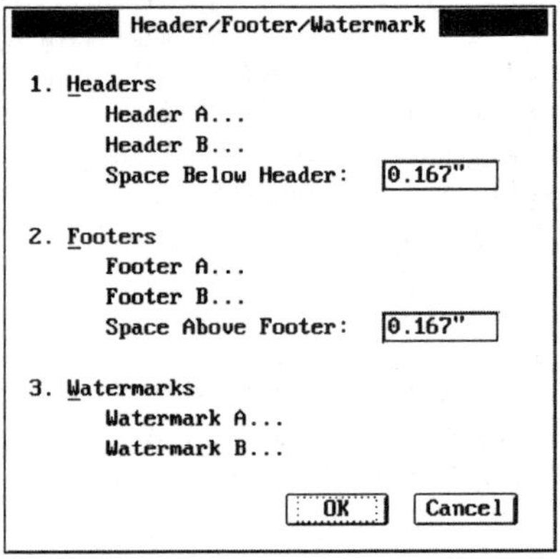

(4) Select Header A by clicking on it and click on the Create button. An empty window appears in which you can type your header text. The status line displays the message *Header A: Press F7 when finished.* In other words, press F7 when you wish to conclude the header.

(5) Enter the following two lines:

```
The Hobbit(Enter)
Page(space)Ctrl-P
```

Pressing Ctrl-P switches on page numbering. The pages are numbered consecutively at the position of this code. You can include the page numbering code in both the header and the footer. This option is an alternative to the Page Numbering feature activated by choosing *Layout* menu, *Page*. Your screen should now look like this:

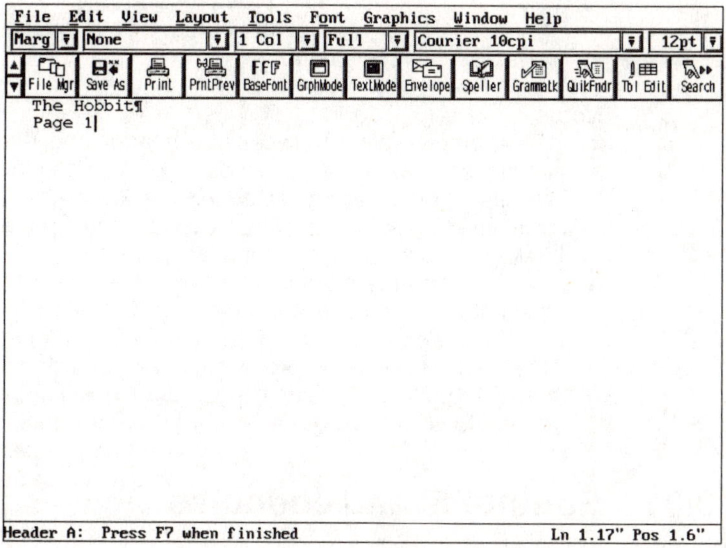

(6) Close the Header window by pressing F7.

We shall also create a footer.

(1) Select the *Header/Footer/Watermark* option from the *Layout* menu.
(2) Activate Footer A by clicking on it. The Footer A box appears. Click on Create.
(3) Type the following lines:

```
Provisional version(Enter)
Glasgow, (space)
```

(4) Add the current date by selecting the *Date* option from the *Tools* menu. Click on *Text* in the submenu.
(5) Close the window by pressing F7.

The text in the header and footer will not be visible on the screen. But you can see headers and footers using the *Print Preview* option from the *File* menu.

(6) Print the text by pressing Shift-F7, 1 to check that you have done everything right.

Notes

- If the empty space between the header and the text is rather less than you would like, you can increase it by selecting *Header/Footer/Watermark* from the *Layout* menu. Then click on the Space Below Header box and enter a larger value.
- You can edit the header by moving the cursor to the right of the code and selecting the *Header/-Footer/Watermark* option from the *Layout* menu. Then select the appropriate header and click on the Edit button. The same procedure is followed for the footer.

9.3 Footnotes and endnotes

Anyone who has to write reports, documentation material, extended essays etc., on a regular basis, will certainly appreciate WordPerfect's footnotes and endnotes capability. You can put all references in the document, acknowledgement of sources and so on, into the notes so there is no disruption to the readability of the document itself.

Footnotes are placed at the bottom of each page, **endnotes** appear at the end of a document. You do not need to concern yourself with note numbering: WordPerfect does this automatically. Nor do you need to work out how much text you can have on a page in order to leave sufficient room for the footnote. WordPerfect puts the footnotes on each page and ends the pages so that there is enough room left over for the footnotes. If you no longer need a footnote, you can simply delete it; WordPerfect automatically modifies the numbering of the other footnotes.

We want to create a footnote in our practice document. First load the document. The description that follows applies equally to creating endnotes.

(1) First move the cursor to the point in the document where the reference number of the footnote is to appear. In this case place the cursor to the right of the last letter in the title.
(2) Select the *Footnote* option from the *Layout* menu. A submenu appears, providing the following possibilities:

Create	This opens the window to create the footnote.
Edit	You can alter existing footnotes by means of this option. When you select this option, specify the number of the existing footnote you wish to modify. The footnote text appears on the screen where you can make alterations.
New Number	Choose this option to give the footnote a different number. This may be necessary for instance if the text is divided over a number of files. In that case, the numbering begins by number 1 each time. This option enables you to specify successive numbering. For example: there are 10 footnotes in file A and 10 in file B. The text will be combined, therefore the footnotes in file B should begin at number 11. Place the cursor at the beginning of file B and click on the New Number option from the *Footnote* submenu. Type 11 in the New Number box and close the window. When you type the text, the numbering will begin automatically at number 11.

Options — We shall discuss this option shortly. It contains important additional facilities for regulating the footnotes.

(3) Click on Create to make a footnote. The text screen for the footnote appears.

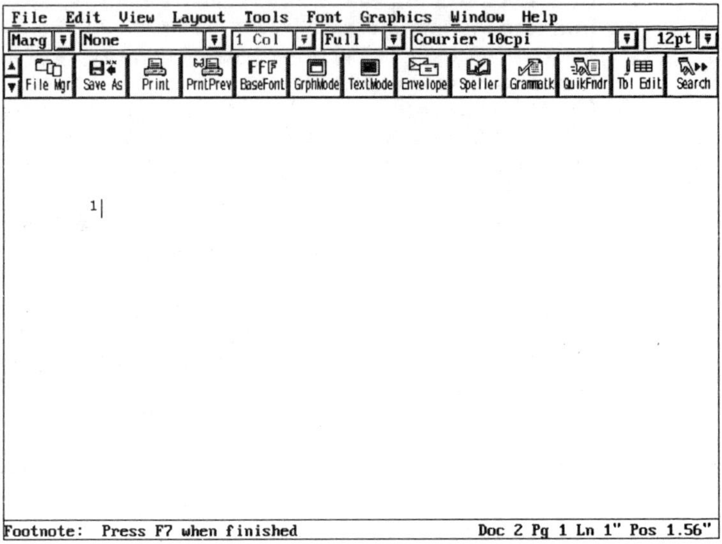

(4) You can now start to define the footnote. To the left of the cursor is the current footnote number. The status line at the bottom indicates that you should press F7 to conclude the footnote.

(5) Type the text for the footnote. You might write:

```
From: J.R.R. Tolkien, The Hobbit.
```

(6) Conclude by pressing F7. The cursor returns to the document, to the right of the footnote character.

You will not be able to view the contents of the footnote on the screen. If you activate the *Print Preview* option from the *File* menu, you will be able to see it in your document.

You can delete footnotes by moving the cursor to the right of the number of the footnote you want to erase and pressing the Backspace key. The text belonging to the footnote is also deleted! If you perform this action unintentionally, select the *Undo* option from the *Edit* menu immediately in order to restore the footnote.

Endnote Placement

If you do not use the Endnote Placement option, WordPerfect will automatically print the endnotes at the end of a file. But it may well be that you have put a number of chapters of a book in just one file and want to have the relevant endnotes printed at the end of each chapter. This facility exists, because the Endnote Placement feature allows you to determine where in the document the endnotes will be printed. This is what you do:

(1) First you must enter the text for the endnotes. This you do in the same way as for footnotes.
(2) Move the cursor to the point where you want the endnotes printed.
(3) Activate the Endnote Placement option by selecting *Endnote* from the *Layout* menu and then *Placement* from the submenu. The question appears on the screen as to whether the endnote numeration should be specified again. It is advisable to answer this question if you wish to make additional endnotes to those already made. If you click on Yes, the numbering of the endnotes will begin again at 1. If you click on No the endnotes will be numbered consecutively. You can make use of this facility if for instance, you have several chapters in one file and you wish to fit the numbering of the endnotes to the chapters. By clicking on Yes, the numbering of the endnotes would begin again at 1.
(4) According to your wishes, click on Yes or No.
(5) A hard page break code and a code for endnote placement is inserted. You can remove the hard page break by deleting the [HPg] code if you do not wish to have the text continue on a separate page.

The Endnote Placement box occupies the same amount of space as the endnote text will occupy in printed form. The endnote, just like the footnote, is not shown on the screen, but you can view it by selecting *Print Preview* from the *File* menu.

The *Options* option in the *Footnote* or *Endnote* submenu enables you to alter the default settings for the creation of footnotes and endnotes. You can determine the appearance of the dividing line between text and footnotes. WordPerfect always places footnotes and footnote texts on the same page. However, if the footnote is extremely lengthy, it may not fit onto one page and may have to be continued on the following page. Just to make it look more sophisticated, you can add the message "continued..." at the end of the relevant page. To do so, select the *Footnote* option from the *Layout* menu. Then choose *Options* and place a cross in the Print Continued Message box.

The settings which are altered using the Footnote Options window only apply to the text which is currently being edited. If you wish to alter one of these settings permanently, select the *Document* option from the *Layout* menu. Then select *Initial Codes Setup*. The Initial Codes window appears. Now select the features that you want to be standard. For instance, while the Initial Codes Setup window is still onscreen, open the *Layout* menu, select *Footnotes* and then *Options*. Click on *Print Continued Message* and click on OK. The code for this function is added to the Initial Codes Setup. Try it out. You can always delete the code by highlighting it using the cursor keys and then pressing Del. Be careful not to delete more than you intend! Otherwise select *Undo* from the *Edit* menu immediately.

9.4 Working on several files at the same time

In WordPerfect you can work on several documents at the same time. This is how you do it:

(1) Load a document (e.g. BILBO) or create a new document.
(2) Load a second document (e.g. BASELINE) or create a new document.
(3) Select the *Switch* option from the *Window* menu. The second document appears on the screen. If you wish to see both documents on the screen at one time, click on the *Tile* option from the *Window* menu.

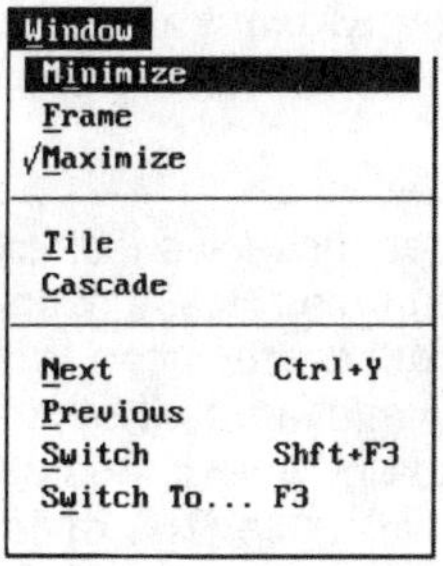

If more files are simultaneously opened, you can choose the file on which you want to work by selecting the *Switch To* option from the *Window* menu. In the subsequent list, click on the name of the file to which you wish to go.

The great advantage of working with several windows at one time is that it becomes easier to copy or move sections of text from one document to another (using the mouse and the Block function).

9.5 Working with styles

So far you have learned a great many ways of determining the appearance of documents, such as setting the margins and line spacing, bold printing of text, centred printing, creating headers and footers etc. If you adhere to the procedures we have described so far, you will have to enter all these formatting instructions manually one after the other, a procedure which can be fairly time-consuming with rather more complicated format settings. By means of the Style function, WordPerfect enables you to enter certain formatting instructions just once and then to store them permanently. You will be creating a **style**. You can retrieve a style at any time and assign it to any document. This document will then be formatted in accordance with the formatting instructions stored in the style. You can enter both formatting and text instructions in a style and a style can also be edited at any time. There are three types of style in WordPerfect:

- **Character styles** are used with blocked text or text you are about to type. This is useful for single words or phrases. A character style is activated at the beginning of the relevant text by means of the [Char Style On] code and is switched off at the end by the [Char Style Off] code. The style definitions do not affect the text before or after these codes.
- **Paragraph styles** affect the paragraph(s) containing the cursor or blocked text. These styles are useful for headings.
- **Open styles** apply to the whole document from the position at which the open style is defined. You switch them on at the beginning of a passage of text and they remain valid for the rest of the text if they are not neutralized by another function.

We shall discuss the Style feature using two examples. We shall create a style for a heading to outline the paragraph style and then an open style for a whole file. We shall again be using the document BILBO, which we originally saved under the name HOBBIT. We shall assume that you have typed the title 'Flies and Spiders' above the text in section 6.3.1.

9.5.1 Creating a paragraph style

First we shall create a paragraph style in which we can store formatting instructions for headings. Although we are initially only applying this style to existing text, in the future we can give every title above every text we type the same appearance. We shall define bold and large letters as features to be used in the formatting instructions for the title.

(1) Select *Styles* from the *Layout* menu. If you have not yet defined any styles, the following window appears:

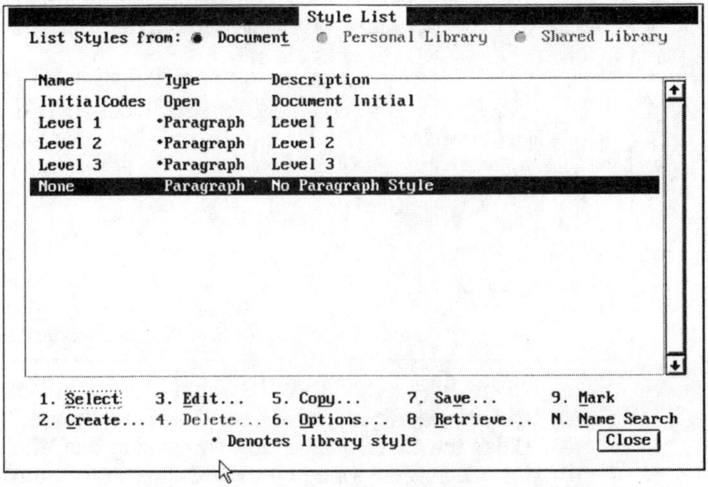

WordPerfect provides a number of defined styles.

(2) We are going to create a style, so click on Create. The Create Style dialog window appears.

(3) First give the style a name of maximum twelve characters for instance 'Title'. Since the Style Type

is already set to Paragraph, you do not need to alter this.

(4) Click on OK. The Edit Style dialog box appears. The more styles you define, the more important it will be to assign a good description to these so that you know exactly which style you require. This description may consist of a maximum of 54 characters. Accordingly, click on the Description box and type *Large and bold letters*.

(5) Click on the Style Contents window. Because we want to print the title in large and bold letters open the *Font* menu and select *Size/Position*. Then choose *Large* from the submenu. The code for Large is placed in the Style Contents window. Then open the *Font* menu again and click on *Bold*. The code for Bold appears in the window.

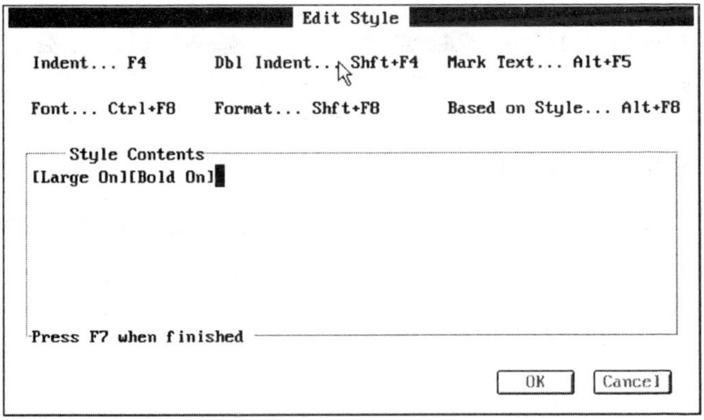

(6) Quit the window by pressing F7.

(7) Close the Edit Style window by clicking on OK.

(8) The Style List window now displays the name of this style, its type and the description (large and bold letters).

(9) Exit this window by clicking on Close.

If you wish to stop working now, save the text using the *Save* command from the *File* menu. The style is saved along with the document.

9.5.2 Working with paragraph styles

Once you have created a paragraph style, you can use it to determine the appearance of passages of text. By way of example we shall format the title above our text:

(1) Move the cursor to the beginning of the document by pressing Home, Home, Cursor Up.
(2) Place the cursor somewhere on the title.
(3) Select *Styles* from the *Layout* list. If you did not leave the text at the end of the previous section, the description of the style you just created should now appear on the screen.
(4) If the style we just created is not already highlighted, do that now by clicking on it or by moving the cursor keys.
(5) Switch on the style by clicking on 1.Select.
(6) The title will appear bold and in large letters.
(7) Save the changes using *Save* from the *File* menu.

9.5.3 Creating an open style

We are now going to create a style you can use to determine the appearance of an entire file. Styles in which line spacing, margins etc. can be specified are particularly suitable for this. We shall create a style in which the line spacing is 1.5 and the left and right margins are 1.5". Since this style is designed for a long document, such as documentation material, we shall also switch on automatic page numbering. Load the practice document BILBO onto the screen again.

(1) Select *Styles* from the *Layout* menu. The list of styles appears on the screen.
(2) As we now want to add a style to this list, select the Create option.
(3) Assign the name 'Document' to the style and select the Open Style by clicking on Style Type to open the pop-up list. Click on OK.
(4) Click on Description in the subsequent Edit Style

box and type: line spacing 1.5 LM1.5", RM1.5", page number 1

(5) Activate the Style Contents box.

(6) Set the line spacing to 1.5 by selecting *Line* from the *Layout* menu. Type 1.5 in the Line Spacing box and click on OK. This setting is imported into the Style Contents box.

(7) Set the margins by selecting *Margins* from the *Layout* menu. Type the value 1.5" in the Left Margin and the Right Margin boxes. Confirm by clicking on OK.

(8) Select the *Page* option from the *Layout* menu and select the Page Numbering section by clicking on it. Click on Page Number Position and click on Bottom Centre. Click on the OK buttons to return to the Edit Style dialog box.

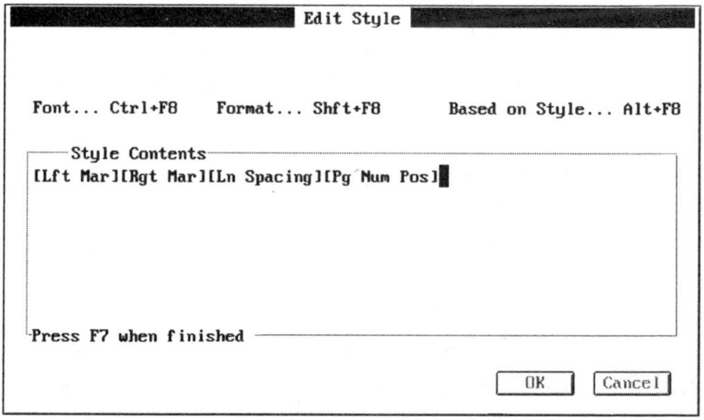

(9) Press F7 to quit this window and then click on OK to return to the Style List window. The name of the style we have just created is now included in the list.

(10) If you also want to use these styles for the appearance of other text files, you will have to save them in a separate file. To do this you select the Save option from the Style List window. In the subsequent Save Styles window, type a name for the file in the Filename box, for instance

STANDRD.STL. You can choose any name you want, providing you observe the general rules for filenames.

(11) You have now saved both the styles in the file STANDRD.STL and you can use them whenever you are working on other documents. All you need to do is load the document to be edited and then activate the styles in the file STANDRD.STL by selecting *Styles* from the *Layout* menu. Then select the *Retrieve* option (nr.8). Type the name of the style file.

(12) Quit the Style List window by clicking on Close.

9.5.4 Working with open styles

We are now going to apply the open style we have just created to the practice document on the screen.

(1) As we want to have the open style apply to the whole document, we move the cursor to the beginning of the document.
(2) Select the *Styles* option from the *Layout* menu.
(3) Move the cursor to the style called Document.
(4) Select this style by clicking on Select. The text is formatted according to the defined style.
(5) Save the document via *Save* from the *File* menu.

9.5.5 Editing styles

You can very easily modify a document whose appearance you have determined by means of a style. This is done by making changes to the style. Proceed as follows:

(1) Load the file whose appearance has been determined with the style.
(2) Select *Styles* from the *Layout* menu.
(3) Move the cursor to the style you want to edit.
(4) Click on Edit.
(5) You can edit the style by deleting unwanted codes

and adding new ones. Remember that a style can also contain text, if you so wish, such as a footnote with a page number for example.

(6) Close the editing process by pressing F7 and clicking on OK.
(7) If you wish, you can also change the edited style on disk by saving it once more.
(8) Return to the text by clicking on Close.
(9) The file is automatically reformatted in accordance with the new codes.

Notes

- If you make a mistake with this exercise, you can repeat it by deleting the codes at the beginning of the document.
- You determine where the style files are to be saved by opening the *File* menu, selecting *Setup*, then *Location of Files*. Normally this is in the WP60 directory but you can change it if required.
- You can also activate styles quickly and easily via the Ribbon. Click on the second box from the left which normally shows None as the default setting.

Exercises

(1) You want to replace the word 'Italy' in a document with the word 'France'. How do you go about it?

____

____

(2) You want to put a one-line footer on every odd page. Write down the steps you must take.

____

____

____

(3) Complete the following: To work with a style you must first define it by selecting the __________ option from the __________ menu. Then select __________. There are three style types in WordPerfect:

a) ______________________________________

b) ______________________________________

c) ______________________________________

________ styles only apply to one or more ________. In contrast, ________ styles apply to the entire document.

Answers

(1) Move the cursor to the beginning of the document. Select the *Replace* option from the *Edit* menu. Search For: Italy; Replace With: France. Click on Replace.

(2) First move the cursor to the beginning of the page. Select *Header/Footer/Watermark* from the *Layout* menu. Click on Footer A. Activate the Odd Pages option and then click on Create. Type the text and conclude by pressing F7.

(3) To work with a style you must first define it by selecting the *Styles* option from the *Layout* menu. Then select *Create*. There are three style types in WordPerfect:
a) *character styles*
b) *paragraph styles*
c) *open styles*

Paragraph styles only apply to one or more *paragraphs*. In contrast, *Open* styles apply to the entire document.

10 Working with macros

In this chapter you will find out about the convenience of macros. You will learn how to define, edit and execute a macro.

10.1 Creating and running macros

The term 'macro' stands for a combined series of commands dealing with recurring and similar operations, such as hyphenating text, saving and printing files, formulating a letter heading or ending etc. You can include both commands and text in a macro and you can use macros when you have to repeat certain series of commands or text input time and again.

To work with a macro there are two things you need to do: first you must **define** the macro, secondly you must **run** the macro.

When you define a macro, you enter manually the commands you want it to contain. WordPerfect keeps these commands on record as it were. Once you have finished, you can run the macro whenever you want at one touch of the key or one click of the mouse.

We shall now create a macro for printing a document on the screen in duplicate. Open the practice document stored under the name BILBO. Switch on the printer and insert paper if necessary.

(1) Activate macro definition by selecting *Macro* from the *Tools* menu. Select *Record*.
(2) Type a name for this macro which we are about to record. When it is saved, this name automatically acquires the extension .WPM. Give it the name TWICE for example so we have an indication of its function.

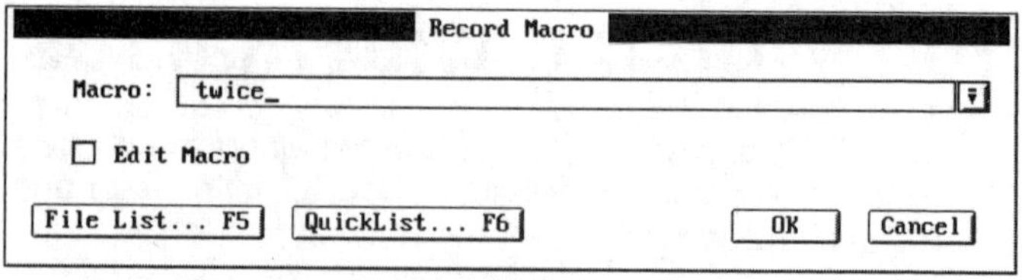

(3) Confirm this by clicking on OK. If a macro with this name already exists, the message 'TWICE.WPM already exists' appears. If you select Replace, the existing macro will be replaced by the new one. If you click on Cancel, you return to the Record Macro window.
(4) When 'Recording Macro' is shown on the status line in the bottom left-hand corner, you can begin specifying the commands or texts which are to be included in the macro.
(5) Select the *Print/Fax* option from the *File* menu.
(6) Place the cursor in the Number of Copies box and type 2.
(7) Click on the Print button to activate the print procedure. Two copies of the text will be printed.
(8) Conclude the recording by selecting *Macro* from the *Tools* menu and then clicking on *Stop*.

Note
If you make a mistake while recording the macro, select *Macro* from the *Tools* option and then *Stop*. Subsequently, repeat the procedure for creating a macro. In that case, click on Replace when the message appears that the macro already exists.

10.1.1 Running the macro

You can run this macro at any chosen moment.

(1) Open a file and switch the printer on.
(2) Select *Macro* from the *Tools* menu and select the *Play* option. The Play Macro dialog box appears on the screen.
(3) Type the name of the macro you wish to run. This

choice can also be made in a more convenient manner by opening the list of available macros. In the Play Macro dialog box, click on the arrow pointing downwards at the right of the Macro text box. The name of the macro we have just created appears in the drop-down list: TWICE.WPM. Double click on this file name.

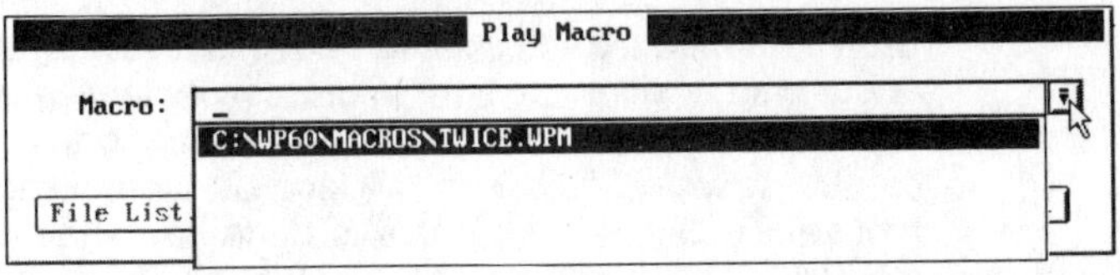

Notes

- Macros are usually stored in the directory which is specially made for them. This directory can be specified in the *Location of Files* box which is opened by selecting *Setup* from the *File* menu. Normally the C:\WP60\MACROS directory is reserved for Macros, keyboard and button bar files. You can specify a different directory if you wish to store these files elsewhere.
- When you are recording macros, only a limited number of mouse functions are available. It remains possible to implement menu commands using the mouse or to click on windows. But for the movements which are not possible you will have to make use of the keyboard.
- You can edit an existing macro whenever you like. Open the macro file, for instance, TWICE.WPM, using the *Macro* option from the *Tools* menu. Select *Record*. Type the name. Then activate Edit. The macro commands appear on the screen where you can edit them.
- When compiling a macro you can assign a key combination to it instead of a name. This may consist of a combination of the Alt key together with a letter of the alphabet, thus Alt-A to Alt-Z. The macro is then saved under the name ALTA.WPM or ALTB.WPM etc. You can then run these macros

by typing the corresponding key combination, such as Alt-A or Alt-B etc.

10.2 Including macros in the button bar

Starting a macro as described above is a rather roundabout way of doing so. It is more convenient to place frequently-used macros on the button bar so that they can be activated quickly by clicking on them using the mouse. To illustrate how this is done, we shall place the TWICE.WPM macro on the button bar. If you do not have this file, create it according to the instructions in the previous section.

(1) Select the *Button Bar Setup* option from the *View* menu. Then click on *Edit*.
(2) Activate the Add Macro function from the subsequent submenu. A dialog window showing all available macros appears.

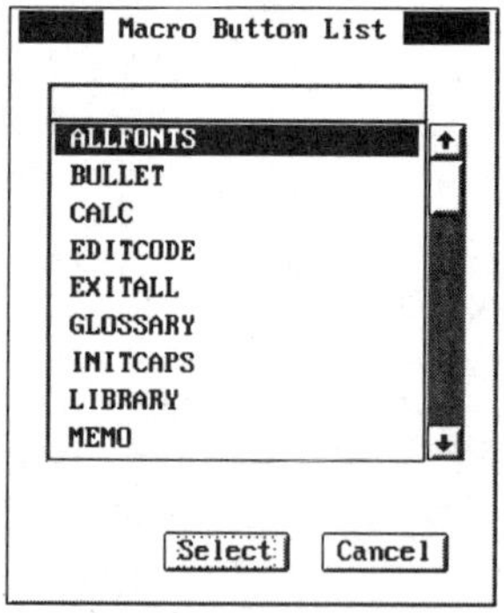

(3) Move the TWICE macro by clicking on the scroll arrow until the appropriate name is highlighted. Click on Select. The new macro button appears at the right of the existing buttons.

(4) Click on OK to return to the text. The macro is shown on the button bar under the name Twice. It can be activated using the mouse.

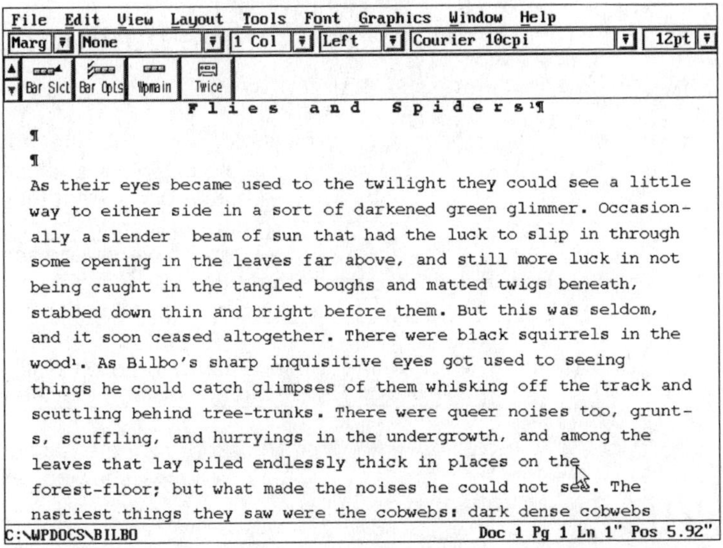

If not all buttons are shown (as is the case here), click on the small triangle pointing upwards at the left-hand side of the button bar to display the other buttons.

Exercises

(1) Create a text macro called 'Ending' containing the following:

```
Yours sincerely,
On behalf of Red Tulip


Peter Fox
```

____

____

(2) How do you start this macro?

____

(3) Under which name is the macro stored on disk?

____

Answers

(1) You have started WordPerfect. The WordPerfect screen is clear and the cursor is at the beginning of the line. You start macro definition by selecting *Macro* from the *Tools* menu. Then select *Record.* Type the name *Ending* and click on OK. As soon as the message *Recording Macro* appears in the status line, type the text:
Yours sincerely, <Enter>
On behalf of Red Tulip<Enter>
<Enter>
<Enter>
Peter Fox <Enter>.
Conclude the recording of the macro by selecting *Tools, Macro, Stop.*

(2) Move the cursor to the position you want the ending to appear. Select *Macro* from the *Tools* menu and then *Play*. Type *Ending* in the Macro text box and click on OK.

(3) *ENDING.WPM*

11 Creating graphics

In this chapter you will learn how to arrange information clearly using the Line Draw feature and how to incorporate graphics created by other graphic programs in WordPerfect files.

11.1 Drawing lines

Using this feature, you can put text inside a box, draw lines on a clear screen or create simple diagrams. To illustrate this, we shall frame a section of text. Because the line drawing feature in combination with proportional fonts does not produce a satisfactory result, it is advisable to choose a non-proportional font such as Courier. Use the *Font* option from the *Font* menu to do this.

(1) The cursor should be at the beginning of an empty file.
(2) As WordPerfect writes over existing text when you use the Line Draw feature, you must be sure that there is enough room on the screen for the lines.
(3) Press the Enter key twice.
(4) Type a space, followed by 'Red Tulip' and then press Enter. This space will be needed for the line.
(5) When the cursor is located just under the text you have just entered, you can activate the Line Draw feature by selecting this option from the *Graphics* menu. The Line Draw dialog box appears.

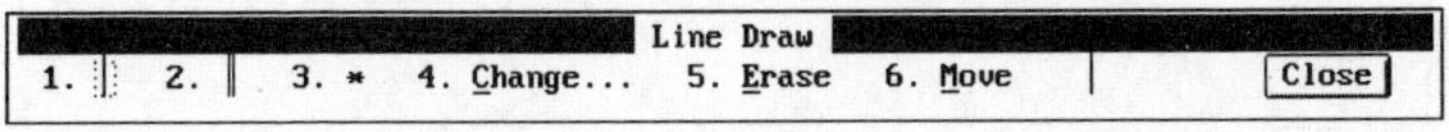

Explanation

1-4 A dialog box appears at the bottom of the window. You can select three different types of line here. Before drawing a line, select one of these types by clicking on it with the mouse. The single line is the default setting. However, there are also other lines available. If you do not wish to use one of these three, click on the fourth option, Change. You can then select a line from the subsequent box.

Erase/Move — As soon as you press one of the four cursor keys, a line will be drawn. If you activate the Move option, the cursor is moved without a line being drawn. If you select the Erase option, characters or lines will be deleted by moving the cursor. By selecting a line type once more, you switch back to the Line Draw function.

(6) — Since the single line is the default setting, you can create a frame around your text immediately. The screen will look something like this.

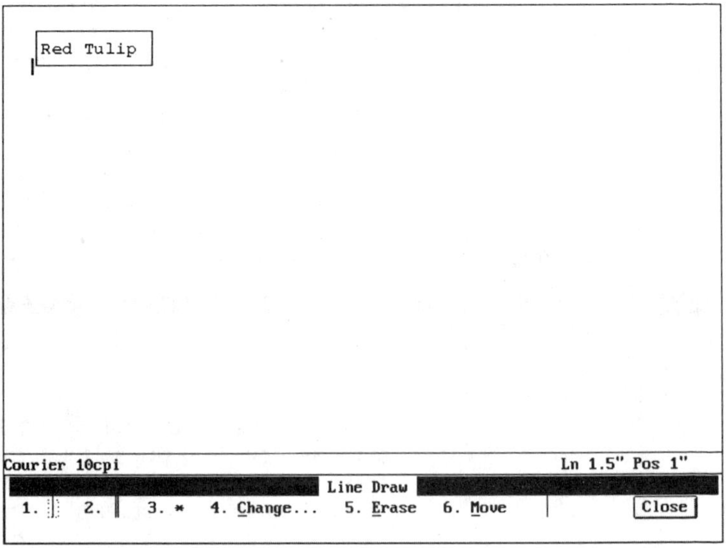

(7) Click on the Close button to quit the Line Draw window.

11.2 Importing graphics into a document

With this feature WordPerfect goes further than conventional word processing and enters a field which was previously the preserve of desktop publishing programs. By desktop publishing we mean the production of very high quality printing using the computer. Using these programs we can add text, figures, tables etc. to a document on the screen. We can now use WordPerfect to give business publications, such as mailshots, company reports, documentation etc. an attractive appearance.

The WordPerfect Graphics feature is not only useful for business purposes of course: you can also use it to put a nice picture on a birth announcement card, for example.

WordPerfect is not a graphic program nor a drawing program. This means that any graphics you want to incorporate in a WordPerfect file must be created in advance using software specially developed for the purpose (graphics programs, drawing programs etc.).

WordPerfect supports a number of graphic programs directly, in other words you can import graphics created using these programs into a WordPerfect file without having to convert them. They include:

file type	**program**
BMP	Window (3.x) and OS/2 Presentation Manager
CGM	Computer Graphics Metafile
DHP	Dr. Halo PIC
DXF	AutoCAD

EPS	PostScript and Encapsulated Post-Script
GEM	GEM Draw
HPGL	Hewlett-Packard Graphics Language Plotter File
PCX	PC Paintbrush
PIC	Lotus 1-2-3 PIC
PNTG	Macintosh Paint
TIFF	Tagged Image File Format
WMF	Windows Metafile Format
WPG	WordPerfect Graphics Format

Images which have been made using other graphic programs can be adopted if you make use of the facility of saving files in a file type which is supported by WordPerfect.

Examples:

- Microsoft Chart files in HPLG file type
- Harvard Graphics files in HPLG, CGM, EPS file types.
- Freelance Plus files in CGM file type.

We shall now give an example of creating a Microsoft Chart file in HPGL file type.

(1) Start up Chart.
(2) Open the file with the graphics image.
(3) Select the HP7475A printer driver.
(4) Print the file to a disk file. This file, created in HPGL file type, can be processed by WordPerfect.

Normally WordPerfect is supplied with more than thirty images. They are stored in files with the extension .WPG, such as GLOBE.WPG etc. These files contain images which can be integrated into a WordPerfect file at any given moment.

Using one of these images, we shall explain how the WordPerfect graphic program can be used.

A graphics image can be imported into a WordPerfect file by placing a graphics box on the screen. This is a box into which we can put text, figures, pictures, etc. We can put a graphics box anywhere in a WordPerfect text file. Here is an example of a graphics box with a figure:

At first sight, what you are about to read may seem rather complicated because of the many options you have in WordPerfect. In fact, importing a graphics image into a file is not difficult. This is what you do:

(1) Load the file into which you want to import the graphics image.
(2) Move the cursor to the place you want to put the graphics image.
(3) Open the graphics image.
(4) If you want another type of setting rather than the WordPerfect default setting, you can edit both the graphics box and the contents of that box, for example a figure.

The picture of the parrot (see the illustration above) is kept in the PARROT.WPG file in the C:\WP60\GRAPHICS directory. We shall import this figure into an empty WordPerfect file by way of practice.

(1) Start WordPerfect. The cursor will now be at the beginning of an empty file.
(2) Open the *Graphics* menu and select the *Retrieve Image* option. The Retrieve Image File dialog box appears.

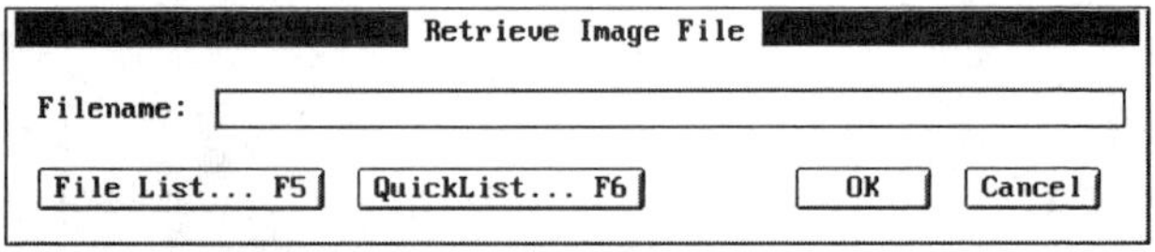

(3) If you do not know the name of the file you wish to import, click on the File List button and confirm the Directory path, C:\WP60\GRAPHICS*.* in the Select List box by clicking on OK. Move through the list of graphic files in the subsequent window until you come to PARROT.WPG.

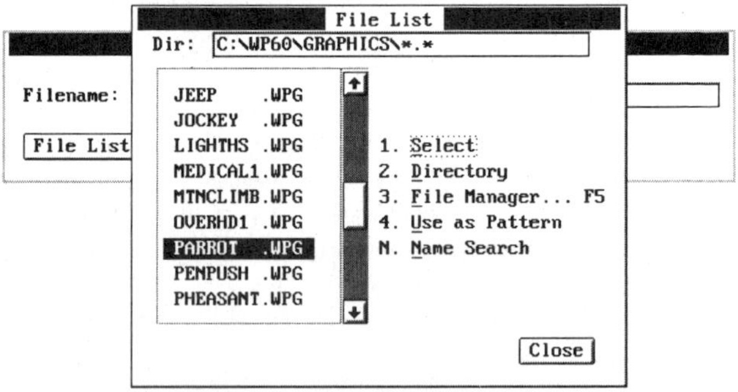

Now click on Select. The image is imported into the current file and appears right-aligned on the screen.

Moving, enlarging and reducing images
You can adjust the position of the image using the mouse. To do so, proceed as follows:

(1) Click on the image which then acquires small square buttons just outside the frame. When you move the mouse across the image, the mouse pointer takes the shape of a four-headed arrow.
(2) Place the mouse pointer on the image and hold down the mouse button. You can now drag the image to a different position. As soon as you release the mouse button, the image is shifted to the new location.

The size of the image is altered as follows:

(1) Click on the image.
(2) Move the mouse pointer to one of the small black squares. It turns into a two-headed arrow. Hold down the mouse button and drag the pointer in the required direction. The buttons enable you to move the frame horizontally, vertically or diagonally. The image is adjusted to fit the frame. You will have to do this according to your own estimation. There are alas no co-ordinates directly available to help you adjust the image as there are in other graphic programs. But you can make exact settings by means of the *Graphics Boxes* option from the *Graphics* menu. Then select *Edit*. The Edit Graphics box appears. This box can also be quickly opened by double clicking on the image.

The Edit Position and Edit Size options in this box enable you to determine the exact position and size of the image.

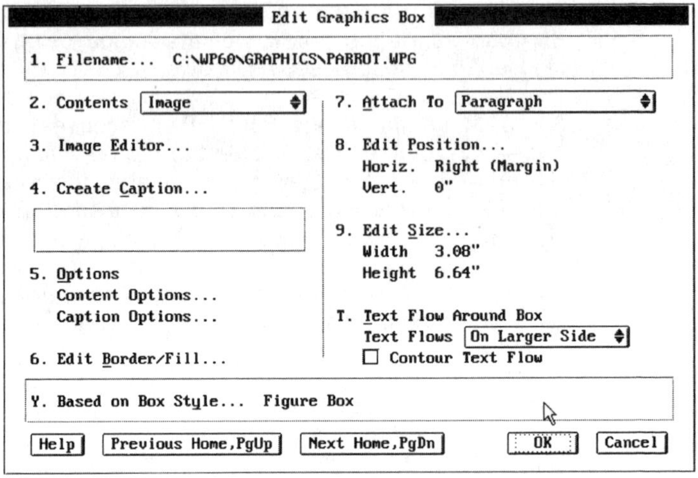

Notes

- If you wish to edit an image in a frame, double click on the image and activate the Image Editor (option 3). You can alter all kinds of settings in the subsequent dialog window. You can also easily adjust many of these options by clicking on the special button bar at the top of the screen. It's worth experimenting now prior to creating a formal document.
- Printing an image is generally more time-consuming than printing text.
- If the print quality of the image is not up to expectation, this may be due to the setting in the Graphics Quality box of the *Print/Fax* option (*File* menu). This may be set to Draft. Change this to High and try again.
- Although we have only outlined how an image is imported into an empty file, you can of course integrate images into text.

Exercises

(1) You want to draw a line graph with double lines. How is this done?

___

(2) You want to import a file called DRAGON.WPG into a WordPerfect file. How is this done?

___
___
___

Answers

(1) Select the *Line Draw* option from the *Graphics* menu. Select the double line as line type. Draw the line by pressing the cursor keys in the appropriate directions.

(2) Select *Retrieve Image* from the *Graphics* menu. Type the name DRAGON in the Filename box. Confirm the command by clicking on OK.

12 Mail Merge: The form letter

In this chapter you will learn how to write 'individual' letters to different people using the Mail Merge feature, while only having to type the basic text once.

12.1 What is a form letter?

The possibilities for form letters are legion: calls for tenders, invitations, mailings to clients, applications, etc.

There are three steps in the creation of a form letter:

- Writing the standard text, in other words, that part of the letter which always remains the same.
- Adding individual, personal elements: address, greetings etc.
- Combining the standard text with the personal elements.

The standard text and the addresses are created in separate files: the standard text in a **form file**, the data to be inserted (name, address, etc.) in a **data file**. In addition to the standard text, the form file also contains the markings for the subsequent insertions.

The secondary file is divided into a number of **records**. A record may consist of a full address along with a salutation, for example.

As you are shortly going to create a secondary WordPerfect file, a sample of such a file is shown overleaf.

name	**address**	**postal code**	**salutation**
Mr Charles Linnaeus	17 Sort Row, Rashult	RO7 1SP	Mr. Linnaeus

A record is made up of different **fields**. In our example the person's name, each part of his address and his salutation each have their own field. How does WordPerfect know where one field ends and another begins? As you can see, we have placed the data in a table. The titles of the columns indicate the limits of the fields. The data which are later to be inserted into the form file are entered in the rows under the column titles.

12.2 Creating a form file

Let's imagine that the travel company Rain Tours wants to remind a group of travellers about a trip it is planning by sending them a personal letter and it is going to use the Mail Merge feature to do this. First it must draft the standard text. Then it must store in a data file the names of the people who are to receive the letters.

In the standard text, which you write first, variables are included for the **name**, the **street**, the **town**, the **postal code** and the **intro**. Rain Tours does, of course, have headed notepaper, but as we cannot permit ourselves such a luxury, we shall have to type in the sender's name ourselves:

(1) Start WordPerfect.
(2) When the clear screen appears, select *Merge* from the *Tools* menu. Select *Define* from the submenu. Select *Form* from the Subsequent Merge Codes dialog window. Confirm your choice by clicking on OK. The cursor is at the beginning of the first line. Type the name of the company:

```
Rain Tours
29 Amazon Street
Old Trafford
Manchester
M16 0XP
```

(3) Now you must mark the place where WordPerfect will later have to put the addressee's name. So press Enter four times.
(4) The cursor is at the beginning of line 10. This is where you put the first marking for the person's name. Select *Merge* from the *Tools* menu, then the *Define* option and click on *Field.*
(5) Now type the name of the first field from the data file: **name.** Confirm this by clicking on OK. On the screen you will see FIELD(name).
(6) The address is to be placed on the next line. So press Enter to move there and select *Merge* from the *Tools* menu. Select *Define* from the submenu and click on *Field.*
(7) Type **address** as the second field name and confirm by clicking on OK.
(8) Compile the letter using the procedure just described. Our example letter should eventually look like this:

```
Rain Tours Ltd.
29 Amazon Street
Old Trafford
Manchester
M16 0XP
(Enter)
(Enter)
(Enter)
(Enter)
FIELD(name)
FIELD(address)
FIELD(postal code)
(Enter)
(Enter)
(Enter)
```

```
(Enter)
Pure adventure: Rain Forest Safari (Enter)
(Enter)
(Enter)
Dear FIELD(intro),(Enter)
(Enter)
Once again this year we would like to extend an
invitation to you to join us on our fantastic
safari to the tropical rain forest in Brazil.
The outward flight will be on the 11th of No-
vember 1994, the return on the 26th of November
1994. The starting point for our journey is Rio
de Janeiro. From there we shall be flying to
the Amazon region. Remember to take not only
comfortable, preferably cotton clothing with
you, but also lightweight rainwear and welling-
ton boots. During the trip you will be staying
in middle class hotels. Unfortunately, we shall
have to charge a supplement for single rooms.
If you have any questions, please get in touch
with our tour leader, Mr Fowler. In the en-
closed folder you will find further details of
the flight from Heathrow and other formalities.
We look forward to seeing you on the 11th of
November.
(Enter)
(Enter)
(Enter)
Yours sincerely,(Enter)
On behalf of Rain Tours Ltd.(Enter)
(Enter)
(Enter)
Percy Thrower(Enter)
```

(9) Now you have finished the text, you can save it under the name RAINTOUR. Clear the screen by selecting *Close* from the *File* menu.

12.3 Creating a data file

You record the addresses in a secondary file. Begin with a new, clear screen.

(1) Select *Merge* from the *Tools* menu. Select *Define* and activate the Data [Table] option.
(2) Click on the Create Table with Field Names option. A dialog window appears in which you can specify the field names (column titles).
(3) Type the first field name, **name**, and confirm this by pressing Enter. Then type the second field name, **street**, and press Enter again. Do the same for the other fields, **town**, **postal code** and **intro**. The dialog window will look like this:

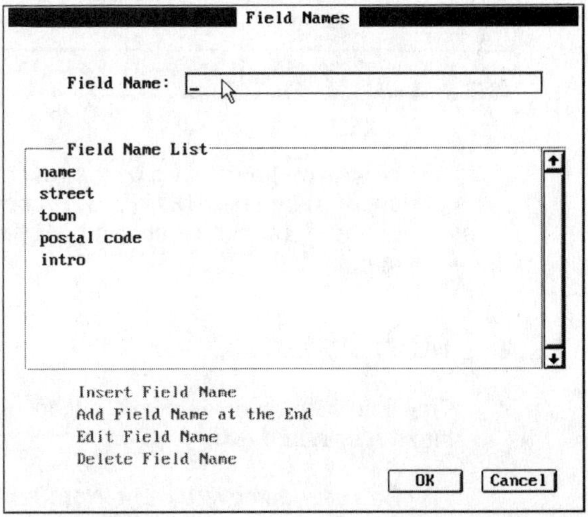

(4) Conclude the registration of the field names by clicking on OK. The cursor appears in the first field under **name**. The data can now be entered in the empty table.
(5) Type the name Gregor Mendel and then move the cursor to the next field by pressing the Tab key. Type the address and the postal code in the same

way. In the last field, type Mr. Mendel. The unchanging part of the intro already exists in the standard text. If you press Tab again, the cursor jumps to the first field in the next row.

(6) Type the rest of the data as shown below:

name	street	town	postal code	intro
Mr. Gregor Mendel	20/22 Fruit Avenue	Hyneston	HY7 22NB	Mr. Mendel
Mr. Julius Sachs	18 Germinate Street	London	L3 2QU	Mr. Sachs
Mr. Stephen Hales	16 Sap Stream	Bekesbourn e	BK7 7TS	Mr. Hales
Mr. Joseph Priestly	17 Leave Green	Leeds	LE3 3PS	Mr. Priestly
Mr. Fred Went	18 Hormone Heights	Amsterdam	1063 JT	Mr. Went

(7) When you have typed all the records, save the file under the name ADDRESS. Remove the contents of the screen by selecting *Close* from the *File* menu.

12.4 Merging

The final step involves the insertion of the addresses into the standard text.

(1) Be sure you have a clear WordPerfect screen.
(2) Select *Merge* from the *Tools* menu. Then select *Run* to actually merge the text and the addresses.
(3) Type the name of the letter file in the Form File box: RAINTOUR.
(4) Type the name of the file containing the addresses in the Data File box: ADDRESS.

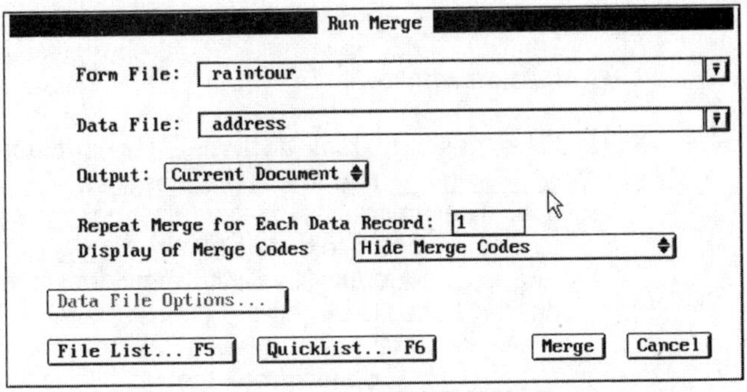

(5) Start the actual merging process by clicking on Merge.

If WordPerfect cannot find the name of the file you enter, it will display an error message. You might have made a mistake in typing the name or accidentally saved the addresses or the standard text under another name. You can examine the names in the list of files to look for the right one.

Merging will take a few seconds. All letters can now be examined. The cursor is now located at the end of the file. Move the cursor to the beginning by pressing Home, Home, Cursor Up. Check to see that all addresses have been inserted correctly and that each letter is on a separate page. Because we have created five letters, this file should contain five letters, each on its own page.

(6) If everything has gone smoothly, you can print the file.

Note
Once you have typed the addresses, you can combine them with any other form file.

Exercises

Complete the following:

(1) The basic text of a form letter is placed in a __________ file, the addresses in a __________ file. The standard text contains not only the unchanging basic text, but also __________, which are subsequently filled with individual items from the address file during the merge.
The variables are placed by means of the __________ option from the __________ menu, then __________, then __________, then __________. Each address in the __________ file forms a __________.

(2) Here is part of a form letter. The bold lines are the variable parts of text. What structure does the form file have?

Mr Charles Correns
Le beau monde
18 Peas Crossing

Munnick
MN6 4LA

Re	Your reference	Our reference	Date
14-04-1994		**MJ/GH**	**16-04-1994**

Answers

(1) The basic text of a form letter is placed in a *form* file, the addresses in a *data* file. The standard text contains not only the unchanging basic text, but also *variables*, which are subsequently filled with individual items from the address file during the merge. The variables are placed by means of the *Merge* option from the *Tools* menu, then *Define*, then *Form*, then *Field*. Each address in the *data file* forms a *record*.

(2) FIELD[name]
FIELD[company]
FIELD[street]

FIELD[town]
FIELD[postal code]

Re	Your reference	Our reference	Date
FIELD[ref]		*FIELD[ourref]*	*FIELD[date]*

13 Columns and tables

In this chapter you will learn the difference between newspaper style columns and parallel columns. We shall also be showing you how to define and use columns. In addition you will learn how to organize text in rows and columns by means of the extensive table function.

13.1 Columns

The Columns feature is one of the most extensive there is in WordPerfect. If you intend producing newsletters, advertising leaflets, information folders, etc., you will certainly appreciate this feature. Column text can be used alongside ordinary text within one file.

WordPerfect makes a distinction between two types of column: newspaper style columns and parallel columns.

You will already be familiar with **newspaper style columns**. As the name indicates, these are columns used in newspapers, magazines and similar publications. The text is usually written in columns, in other words, once a column is full, the text automatically continues at the top of the page in the next column.

You use **parallel columns** when two or more adjacent columns have a direct link in terms of content, as is often the case, for example, with translations, budgets, lists, etc. In this case, in contrast to newspaper style columns, the text does not run continuously from one column to the next. A classic example of parallel columns is the translation. The original text appears in the left-hand column, for example, with the translation on the right. The illustration overleaf shows an example of newspaper style columns.

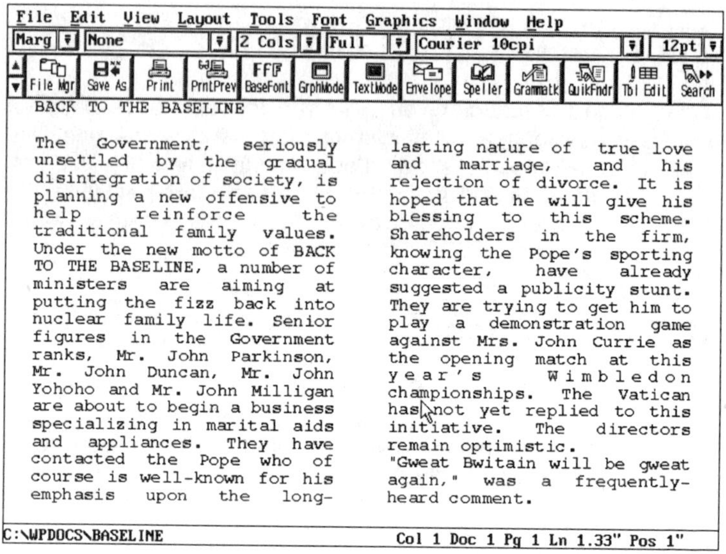

There are three stages to writing text in columns: first you must define the columns, then you switch on the Columns feature and finally you type the text. As an example we shall create a document with newspaper style columns.

13.2 Defining columns

We shall demonstrate this feature using the BILBO document and put the text into two columns.

(1) Open the document called BILBO.
(2) Place the cursor at the beginning of the text. We do not wish the column function to be disturbed in any way by any superfluous codes, so delete all the style codes you applied during the exercises in chapter 9.
(3) Move the cursor to the beginning of the text after the title. As the margin settings also have an effect on the columns - the narrower the margins, the less text will fit in the columns - check that both the

left and right margins are set to 1", which is in fact the default setting. If this is not the case, you can set the margins to the said positions.

(4) The preparatory steps are now complete. We can move on to defining the columns. In the definition we specify the type of column, the number of columns etc. To do this you select the *Columns* option from the *Layout* menu. The following dialog box appears on the screen:

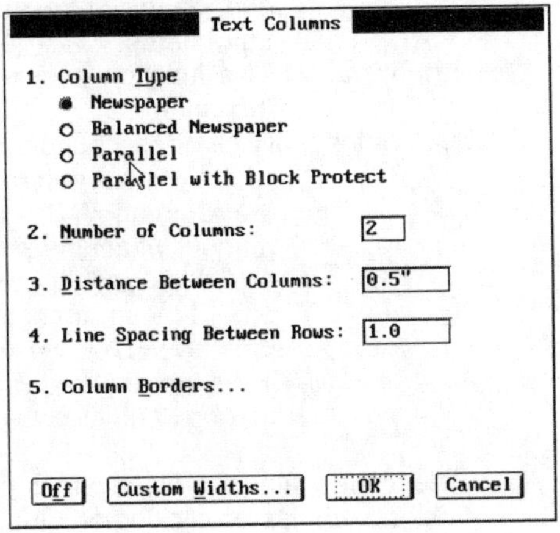

Explanation

Column Type
: This option is used to determine the type of column. Normally that is the newspaper style. Select Balanced Newspaper if the text has to be divided evenly between the columns. If Parallel with Block Protect is chosen here, paragraphs will not be split by a page break. If a page break is really necessary, the whole column is placed on the next page.

Number of Columns
: This determines the number of columns. WordPerfect is capable of displaying 24 columns per page; the

	default setting is 2. If, for example, you wish to have four columns, type 4 in this box.
Distance Between Columns	Determines the distance between the columns. The default setting is 0.5". Increase it or decrease it to meet your own requirements.
Line Spacing Between Rows	Normally WordPerfect places one blank line between two columns underneath one another. You can also change this setting to meet your requirements.
Column Borders	This function draws a frame around the columns.
Custom Widths	Click on this button to adjust the line width of the different columns. In the Column Width dialog box, the number of columns and their widths are displayed. If you wish to alter one of these, mark the relevant column and click on the Edit button. Type the required width in the Width text box and click on OK.

(5) Select the Balanced Newspaper option and confirm your choice by clicking on OK.
(6) If the title is still by any chance left-aligned, centre it so that it appears above both columns.

Notes

- If you wish, you can place the cursor at the end of the file and then switch the column function off. Select *Columns* from the *Layout* menu and then click on the Off button in the Text Columns dialog box. The text which you subsequently type is then laid out in one column again as usual. You can switch the column function on and off as you please in a document.
- There are special rules for moving the cursor within the column function. The key combinations Alt-Cursor Right and Alt-Cursor Left enable you to switch to the right or to the left column respectively.

When working with **parallel columns** you can proceed, in principle, in the same way as described above. You define the columns, switch the column function on and enter text. The only difference is that WordPerfect only switches to the next column when you type Ctrl-Enter. Just to complete the information, we shall describe how you should proceed when working with parallel columns.

(1) Column definition: under Column Type, select Parallel instead of Newspaper. If one of the columns is to be narrower than the other, the default settings are not applied. Any alterations are made by means of the Custom Widths button.

(2) Entering text: type the first line of the text for the first column.

(3) Then type the text for the second column. You move to the second column by pressing Ctrl-Enter. By pressing Ctrl-Enter, you switch to the next item in the first column, and so on.

You can also define columns quickly and easily using the Columns button from the Layout button bar. The Layout button bar is activated by clicking on the small triangle pointing downwards at the extreme left-hand side of the normal button bar. Click on *Bar Slct*. A list of available button bars appears. Double click on Layout. The new bar appears along the top of the screen.

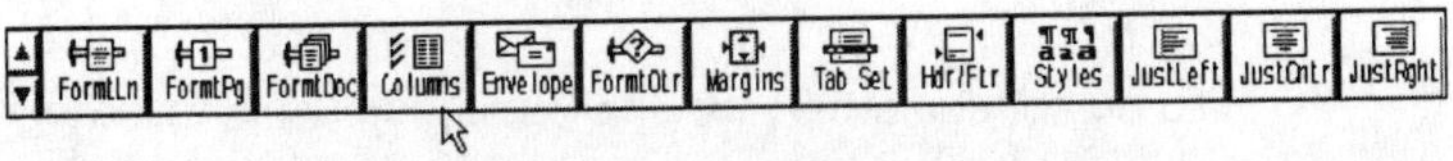

Click on the button and specify the required number of columns in the Text Columns dialog box.

13.3 Tables

A table consists of columns and rows containing data. We shall first introduce a number of terms used when discussing this topic. Examine the table overleaf.

Table structure

A1	B1	C1
A2	B2	C2
A3	B3	C3

A table consists of rows, columns and cells. A cell is the smallest unit in the table and is actually the intersection between column and row. The first cell in a table, A1, is situated at the junction of the first column and the first row. The position of a cell is indicated by a letter for the column and a number for the row. The columns are designated from left to right by letters of the alphabet, and the rows by numbers from top to bottom. Thus B2 is in the second column on the second row. This is also referred to as a cell *address* and this address is often used in calculation functions with cell data. The table above consists of three columns and three rows, producing nine cells.

There are three stages in working with tables:

- creating the table
- processing the data (entering text and numbers in the cells)
- editing the table (formatting cells, rows and columns).

To demonstrate this, we shall outline how the following table is constructed.

company	**turnover 92 (x1000)**	**turnover 93 (x1000)**
Rain Tours	300	410
Snow Tours	230	290

We shall proceed as follows. We shall first create an empty table. Then we shall enter text and numbers and finally we shall format the entire table.

13.3.1 Creating the table

First place the cursor at the position in the text where the table is to be inserted. In this case, we shall create the table in a new, empty document.

(1) Start up WordPerfect. The cursor is at the beginning of the document.
(2) Select the *Tables* option from the *Layout* menu. Select *Create* from the subsequent submenu. The Create Table dialog box appears.
(3) The default setting in the Columns box is 3. Type 3 here if that is not the case. Change Rows to 3 as well. The numbers can be increased by clicking on the small triangle pointing upwards.
(4) Click on OK to confirm these specifications.

Notes

- It is advisable to set the margins to the required positions prior to creating the table. This is done using the *Margins* option from the *Layout* menu. This is because the width of the columns is geared to the margin settings. If you alter the margins later, the column width is not automatically adjusted to the new values. If, however, it becomes necessary to change these values, the column width can be altered as follows:

(1) Place the cursor in one of the table cells.
(2) Select *Tables* from the *Layout* menu and select *Edit* from the submenu.
(3) Select the second option in the subsequent settings window. The Column Format dialog window appears. Here you can specify the new width.

- A table can be deleted by moving the cursor to the beginning of the table and then activating the Reveal Codes function by pressing F11 or selecting *Reveal Codes* from the *View* menu. Move the cursor to the appropriate code, [Tbl Def], and press Del.

- When creating a table, WordPerfect makes use of certain default settings (double line for the borders etc.) which can be altered if you wish (*Layout, Tables, Create, Create Table OK, 6.Lines/Fill*).
- If you place the cursor in a table cell, you can alter the width of the columns by selecting *Tables* from the *Layout* menu, then *Edit*. The column width can then be altered by pressing Ctrl-Cursor Left and Ctrl-Cursor Right.

13.3.2 Entering data

We shall now enter the data. The table which we have just created is displayed across the entire width of the screen. If you have not yet moved the cursor, it will be positioned in the first cell of the table. Otherwise move the cursor to the first cell. This can be done using the mouse but there are also key combinations available for this task:

Tab	one cell to the right
Shift-Tab	one cell to the left
Alt-Cursor Right	one cell to the right
Alt-Cursor Left	one cell to the left
Alt-Cursor Up	one cell upwards
Alt-Cursor Down	one cell downwards

As long as no text has been entered, you can move the cursor from one cell to another using the normal cursor keys.

(1) Now type the text in the table. If necessary, move the cursor to the first cell. The status bar should display 'Cell A1'.

(2) Type the titles of the columns first. Press Ctrl-B, type Company and press Ctrl-B again. Press Tab to move to the next cell.

(3) Type the title for the second column: press Ctrl-B, type Turnover 92, press Ctrl-B. Press Enter and type (x1000). As you see, the cursor moves to the next line in the cell and not to the next line of the table. WordPerfect allows several lines within one cell. The cell height is then adapted to the number of lines.

(4) Type the rest of the table as illustrated above. Press Tab to move to the next cell.

Notes

- Most functions for formatting and editing text (marking, bold, underlining, copying, setting tabs etc.) are also available when working with tables.
- If you wish to place a tab stop in a cell, press Home and then Tab if you want to have a left-aligned tab. If you want a right-aligned tab, press Home, Alt-F6. Press Home, Shift-F6 for a centred tab and Home, Ctrl-F6 for a decimal tab.
- In addition to text you can also place images in a cell. In a table consisting for instance of two columns and one row, you could place an image in the first cell and an explanatory text in the other. To do this, proceed as follows: create the table (2 columns, 1 row). Place the cursor in the cell which is to contain the image and import the image as outlined in section 11.2.

13.3.3 Editing the table

There are many facilities available to edit the table. You can for example:

- adjust the column width and row height
- add and remove columns and rows
- format the borders of the cells and columns
- format the cell contents.

We shall now make some changes to the table we have just created:

a) We shall add an extra row containing data from

the Hill Tours company.

b) We shall delete the second column containing the obsolete data from 1992.

c) The left column must remain left-aligned, but the turnover figures and the corresponding title are to be centred.

d) The column titles are to be clearly separated from the rest of the table by a thick dark line.

Inserting rows

We shall first insert an extra row for the data concerning Hill Tours. We wish to make an alphabetical table, thus the Hill Tours data should be placed before Rain Tours, at the top of the table.

(1) Place the cursor on the second row of the first column. The status bar indicates Cell A2.

(2) Normally rows and columns are inserted, respectively, above and to the left of the current cursor position. Select *Tables* from the *Layout* menu and then select *Insert Row*.

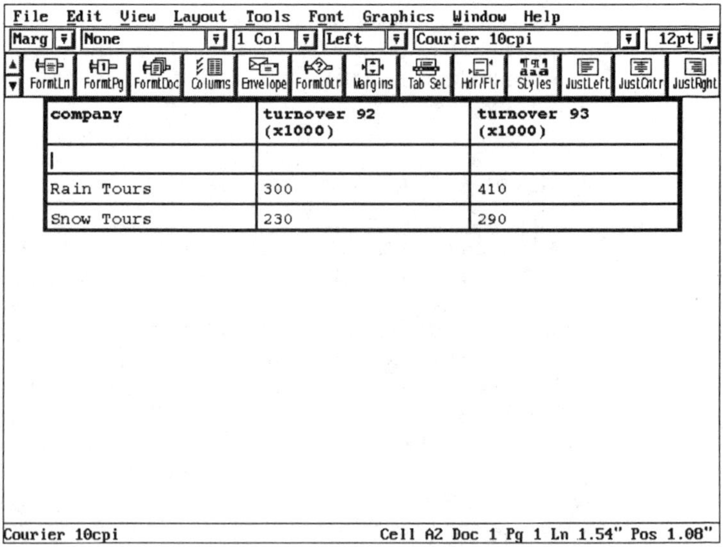

The new row will be inserted above the currently active row. Data above are moved upwards. You can also press Ctrl-Ins instead of selecting from the menu. If you press Ctrl-Plus (from the numeric keypad), you can insert a row *under* the currently active row. This is convenient for instance if the cursor is located on the last row of a table and you wish to add another row.

Deleting columns

We shall now remove the column containing the obsolete data from 1992.

(1) Move the cursor to the column with the unwanted data, B1 in this case.

(2) Select *Tables* from the *Layout* menu and then *Edit*. Click on the Del button at the bottom of the screen. Select Columns In the subsequent Delete box. Specify 1 in the How Many? text box. Click on OK. Quit the Edit Table box by clicking on Close. The second column is now deleted. If you have second thoughts, you can restore it now by clicking on *Undo* from the *Edit* menu.

Formatting columns and cells

We shall now centre the title of the turnover column and the corresponding data.

(1) Ensure that the cursor is located in the table and select *Tables* from the *Layout* menu. Select *Edit*.

(2) Mark column B by dragging the mouse downwards over it.

(3) Then click on the second option at the bottom of the screen, Column. Click on Centre in the Alignment section of the subsequent Column Format box.

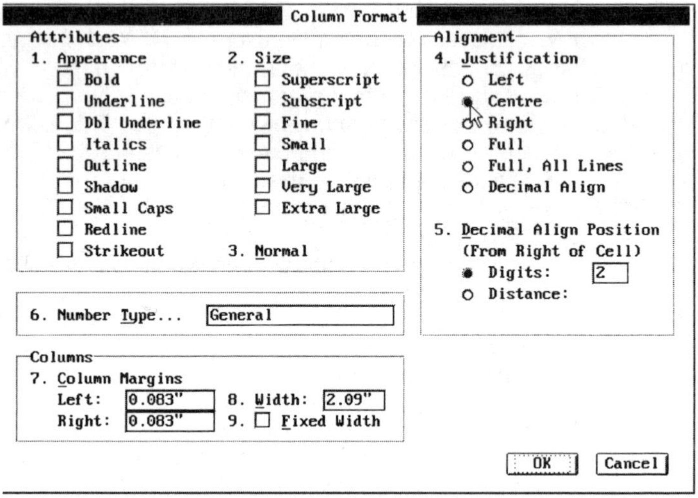

(4) Confirm this by clicking on OK and return to the document by clicking on Close in the Edit Table box.

Altering the table border

Finally, we shall create a distinct separation between the table title and table data.

(1) Place the cursor in the first cell on the second row, A2.
(2) Select *Tables* from the *Layout* menu and then *Edit.*
(3) The thickness of the line is to be altered across the entire width so mark the row by dragging the mouse across it.
(4) Click on the sixth option at the bottom of the screen, Lines/Fill.
(5) Click on Top and then on Thick Line in the subsequent Line Styles box. Confirm your choice by clicking on Select.

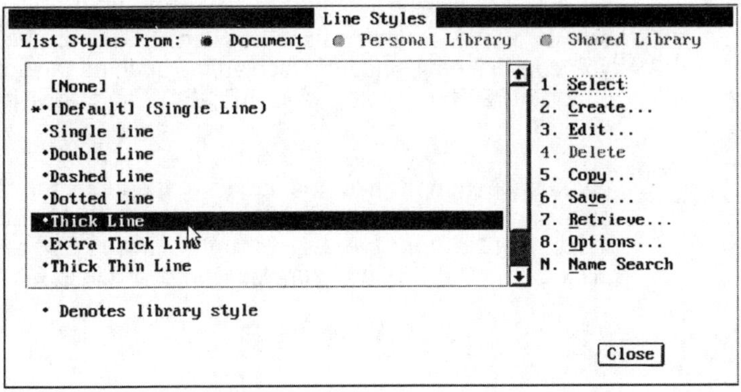

(6) Close the Table Lines box by clicking on Close and do the same in the Edit Table box.

Notes

- You can also make calculations using this table. We shall demonstrate this using our current example. The Hill Tours company had a turnover of 330,000 pounds in 1993. Place the cursor in the last row of the table and press the Ctrl-Plus key (numeric keypad) to add a row to the table. Move the cursor to the last cell of the table (B5) and select *Tables* from the *Layout* menu. Select *Edit* and activate the fifth option, Formula. The Table Formula box appears:

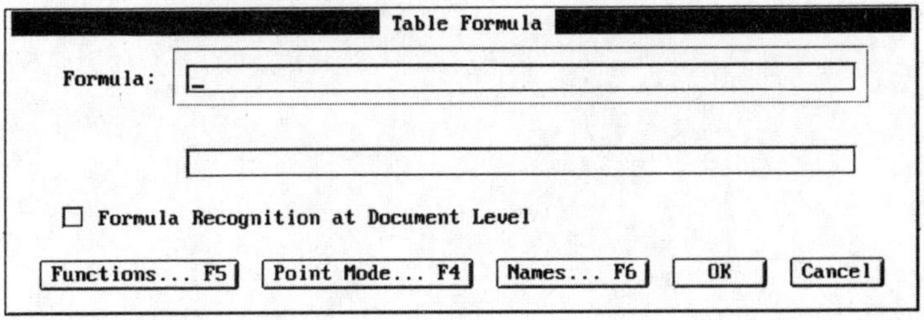

We wish to add the various turnover figures. To do this, type the formula in the Formula box: B2+B3+B4. Close the box by clicking on OK. In the table, the result is shown at the current cursor position, B5. Of course, you can make all kinds of calculations such as multiplication (B2*B3), subtraction (B3-B4) and division (B2:B3).

If you subsequently alter the figures in the table, the result is not automatically adjusted. To bring it up to date, select *Tables* from the *Layout* menu, select *Edit* and click on the Calc button to implement recalculation.

Exercises

(1) Complete the following: WordPerfect makes a distinction between two types of column: __________ columns and _________ columns. _________ columns are highly suited to translations, indexes, etc., while _________ columns are used for articles, drafting, etc. There are two stages involved in working with columns:

a) ____
b) ____

The first stage, ____________________, is carried out by selecting *Columns* from the *Layout* menu. In this stage, you define the _________ of column and the __________ of columns. After the definition stage you can type the text which is to be entered. You can switch off the column function by selecting __________ from the __________ menu and then clicking on the ___________ button.

(2) We want to print a document in three parallel columns. Write down which commands you will use to define the columns.

____

(3) How do you move to a new column when working with parallel columns?

____

(4) Complete: A table consists of ___________, ___________ and cells.

(5) Write down the commands used to create a table consisting of two columns and four rows.

____

(6) The contents of cell B1 in a table are to be displayed in boldface. How is this done?

____

Answers

(1) WordPerfect makes a distinction between two types of column: *newspaper style* columns and *parallel* columns. *Parallel* columns are highly suited to translations, indexes, etc., while *newspaper style* columns are used for articles, drafting, etc. There are two stages involved in working with columns:

a) *column definition*
b) *entering text*

The first stage, *column definition*, is carried out by selecting *Columns* from the *Layout* menu. In this stage you define the *type* of column and the *number* of columns. After the definition stage you can type the text which is to be entered. You can switch off the column function by selecting *Columns* from the *Layout* menu and then clicking on the *Off* button.

(2) Select *Columns* from the *Layout* menu. Type 3 in the Number of Columns box. Activate the Parallel option in the Column Type list and click on OK.

(3) By pressing *Ctrl-Enter*.

(4) A table consists of *columns, rows* and cells.

(5) Select *Tables* from the *Layout* menu and select *Create*. Type 2 in the Columns box and 4 in the Rows box. Conform this by clicking on OK and close the Edit Tables box by clicking on Close.

(6) Select *Tables* from the *Layout* menu and then *Edit*. Mark cell B1. Activate option 1 Cell at the bottom of the screen and click on the Bold check box in the Attributes list in the subsequent Cell Format box. Click on OK. Quit the Edit Tables box by clicking on Close.

14 Other programs

In this chapter you will find out about the possibilities and the limitations of the WordPerfect spelling check program and how to make use of the thesaurus.

14.1 Spelling check

Do not expect too much from the spelling check feature. It is not the case that you can use the WordPerfect speller program to remove all the spelling mistakes from your document and that you will therefore never again need to check your work. WordPerfect checks the spelling against a dictionary. If it comes across a word it does not know in the document, it highlights the word and in some cases suggests alternatives. Since the size of this dictionary is limited, it will often happen that WordPerfect will display a word that is actually a perfectly good one. And it will not recognise mistakes such as 'I walks' because both 'I' and 'walks' appear in the dictionary.

Since the spelling checker is convenient but also restricted, we shall not dwell on this particular feature for too long. We shall simply show you how you can check the spelling in a document.

(1) Start WordPerfect and open the file whose spelling you want to check.
(2) Select *Writing Tools* from the *Tools* menu and select *Speller*. The relevant dialog window appears.

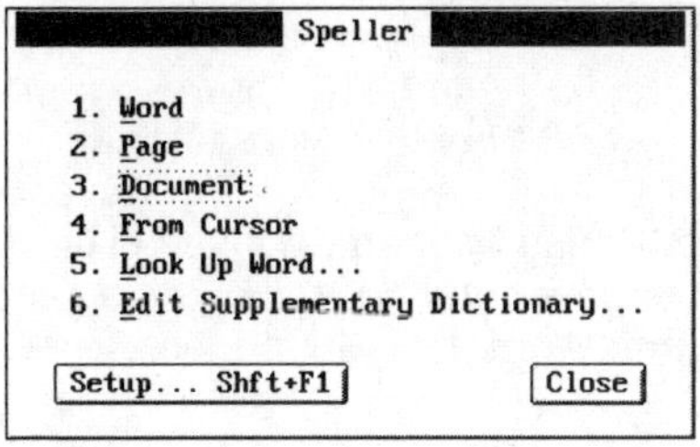

Explanation

Word	If you specify this option, WordPerfect will check the word at the current cursor position.
Page	The page in which the cursor is currently situated will be checked.
Document	The entire document will be checked.
From Cursor	The text will be checked from the current cursor position onwards.
Look Up Word	If you select this option, a dialog box appears in which you can specify words or word patterns which do not exist in the current text. These are then checked. Type the word in question in the Word or Word Pattern box. When you press Enter, WordPerfect will show a list of words corresponding to that pattern. By making use of wildcards, such as the question mark representing one letter or an asterisk representing a string of letters, you can look for certain patterns. For instance the pattern 't*k' will find words ranging in length from 'talk' to 'thunderstruck'. On the other hand, if you type 't??k', words of the same length appear, such as 'talk', 'tick', 'tusk' etc.
Edit Supplementary Dictionary	This option enables you to make alterations to the supplementary list of words.
Setup	If you click on this button, you can make alterations to the default settings in the WordPerfect speller. Normally, however, you will not need to alter anything.

(3) Select Document here. If the speller encounters a word or pattern that does not appear in the dictionary, the Word Not Found box appears on the screen.

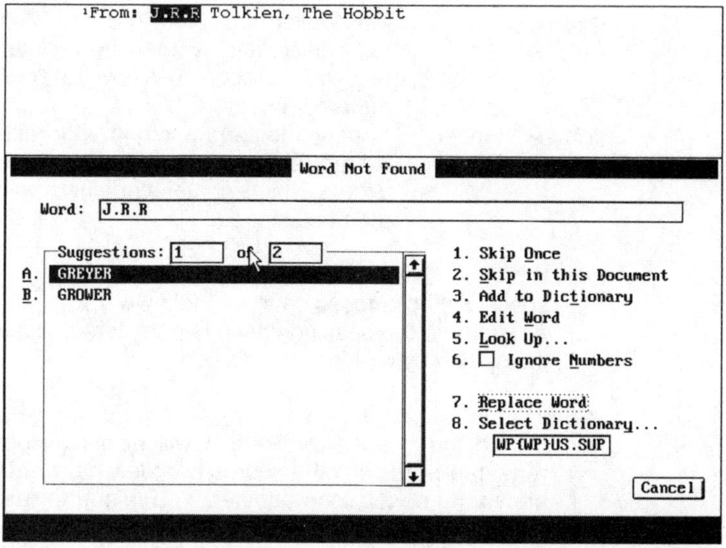

According to WordPerfect, this word pattern is incorrect. Alternatives will appear in the Suggestions section. If you wish to adopt one of these, mark the word and click on Replace Word. You can also change the word yourself by clicking on Edit Word and then making the appropriate changes. If the word is correctly spelled after all, select one of the following options:

Skip Once	This indicates that you do not wish to alter the word. If the WordPerfect speller encounters this word again further on in the text, it will be marked again.
Skip in this Document	This also indicates that you do not wish to alter the word. Now you wish WordPerfect to ignore any subsequent occurrences in this document.
Add to Dictionary	This option adds the word to the WordPerfect dictionary. During the rest of this check and in any other checks of other documents, it will be regarded as being correct.

Look Up	This option indicates that you wish to replace this word with another but you do not know how to spell the other word.
Ignore Numbers	If many numbers occur in your text, it is advisable to activate this option. Words which contain numbers will then be skipped.

(4) When you have selected one of these options, the spelling check moves on to the next word.
(5) As soon as the spelling check is completed, close the speller by clicking on OK.

Notes

- During the check WordPerfect will also highlight repeated words, in other words two identical words appearing next to one another. You might, for example, have accidentally typed the word 'and' twice.
- New words added are stored in a file called WP{WP}UK.SUP. You can edit this file via the *Writing Tools* option from the *Tools* menu. Then select *Speller* and *Edit Supplementary Dictionary* in the subsequent dialog box.
- You can also activate the spelling check by clicking on the Speller button on the button bar. If this is not shown, open the *View* menu, select *Button Bar Setup* and click on Select. Highlight WPMAIN and click on Select. The appropriate button bar is installed.

14.2 Thesaurus

You can use the **thesaurus** if you cannot think of the right word when you are typing text. The thesaurus gives you a list of alternatives for a given key word. These alternatives can be both synonyms, that is, words with the same meaning, and antonyms, words with an opposite meaning. If you feel that a certain word is appearing too often in your document, you can use the thesaurus to see which other words you might be able to use instead.

We are now going to show you how the thesaurus works using the example of the adjective 'beautiful'. Type 'beautiful'.

(1) Type *beautiful*.
(2) Place the cursor on the word and activate the Thesaurus by selecting *Writing Tools* from the *Tools* menu.
(3) The screen will look like this:

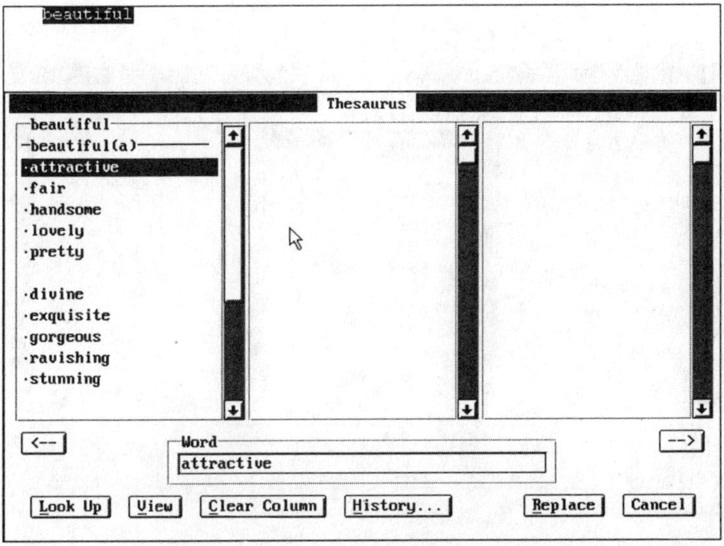

The word *beautiful* is shown inversely at the top of the screen and again at the top left-hand corner of the Thesaurus box. Immediately under this, you see *beautiful (a)* which indicates that the words shown are synonyms of the adjective *beautiful*. This is useful to know in cases where a word can be used as a verb, adjective or noun so you can choose from the proper category. If you click on the scroll arrow pointing downwards, you will come to *beautiful (ant)* which gives antonyms (opposite meaning) for this word.

The words in the list which have a dot next to them can be used to search further. You 'dig deeper' as it were, in one particular direction.

(4) The word *attractive* is highlighted. It also has a dot in front of it. Double click on this word to produce a list of synonyms for this word. This is shown in the second column.

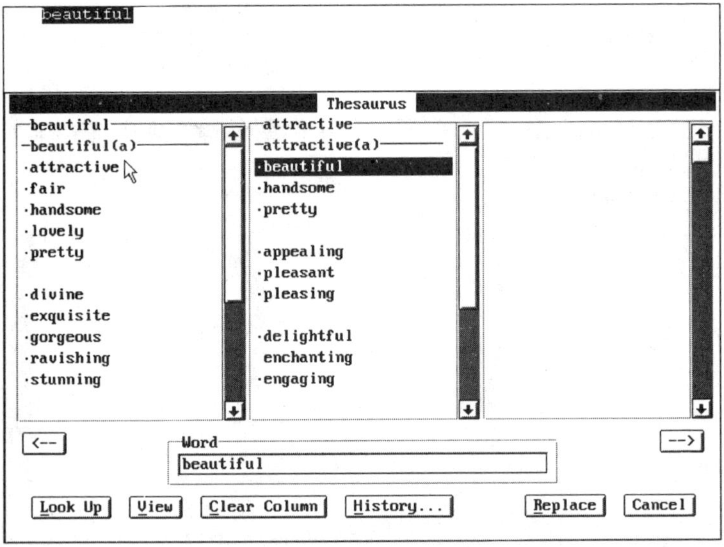

This column also contains words with a dot in front of them. Double click on *handsome* to activate a third list.

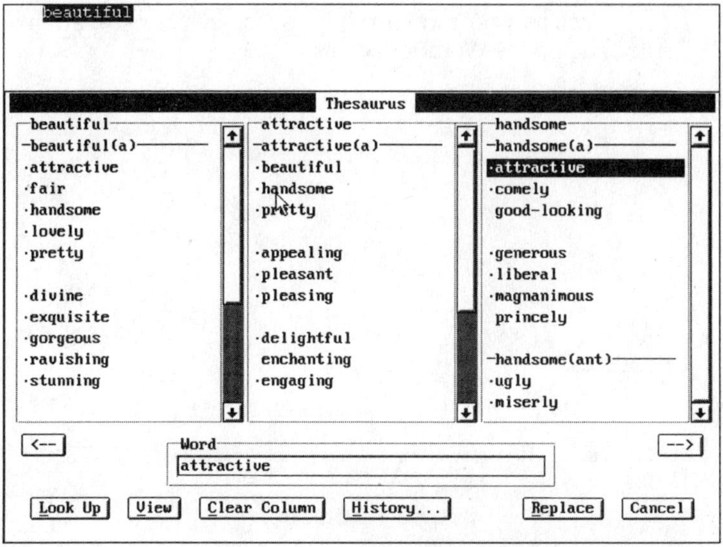

It is possible to click on any word preceded by a dot in order to activate more lists. Since only three columns can be shown on the screen, you switch from one list to another by clicking on one of the arrow buttons (← or →).

(5) We shall replace the word *beautiful* which is still marked, with the word *comely*. Click on this word, which then appears in the Word box at the bottom of the window.
(6) Click on the Replace button.

The window is closed and the word *beautiful* is replaced by the word *comely*.

Note
As far as this particular aspect is concerned, word processing is clearly still in its infancy. The words appearing in the lists of alternatives often cannot simply be inserted into the document because they do not suit the context. If you find that working with the thesaurus produces unsatisfactory results, you may be better off

racking your own brains for synonyms rather than relying on the WordPerfect thesaurus.

Exercises

(1) You want to check the spelling on a certain page. What do you do?

____

(2) You want to see a list of alternatives for the key word 'give' on the screen. How do you do that?

____

____

Answers

(1) Place the cursor at the relevant page. Select *Writing Tools* from the *Tools* menu and then select *Speller*. Activate the *Page* option.

(2) Place the cursor on the word *give*. Select *Writing Tools* from the *Tools* menu and select *Thesaurus*.

15 Installation of the program and printer selection

In this chapter you will learn what you must do before you start working with WordPerfect for the first time and how you can tailor the default settings in WordPerfect to your own individual requirements.

15.1 Installation

WordPerfect 6.0 is supplied on seven 3.5 inch diskettes. Four of these are installation diskettes and three are program diskettes. We shall now describe how to install WordPerfect 6.0 from these diskettes to your computer harddisk.

(1) Switch on the computer. The MS-DOS prompt must indicate that you are in the root directory: C:\. If this is not the case type the command **cd ** which will move you to the proper directory.
(2) Insert the **Install 1** diskette in diskdrive A: or B:.
(3) Switch to this disk drive by typing A: or B: behind the DOS prompt.
(4) Start the installation program by typing the **Install** command and pressing **Enter**.
(5) First you have to specify whether or not you have a colour monitor. If red, green and blue boxes are displayed on the screen, reply by typing **Y**es, otherwise **N**o.

The installation menu now appears on the screen.

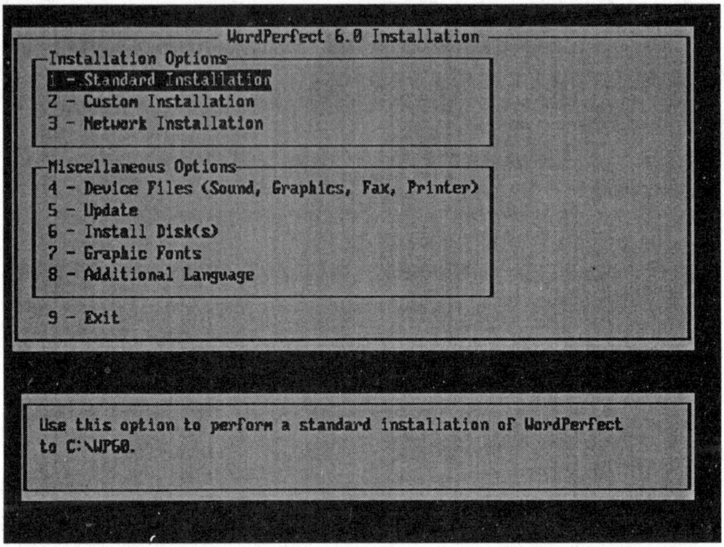

The *Standard Installation* option is already selected. This installation will lead to a complete installation of WordPerfect 6.0 in the default directories C:\WP60, C:\WP60DOS etc. which are suggested by WordPerfect 6.0. If these directories do not exist as yet, the installation program creates them. If you wish to accept the standard installation, press **Enter**. This is normally sufficient for most users, but if you wish, you can place the WordPerfect 6.0 files in the directories and drives of your choice by choosing the *Custom Installation*.

(6) If you accept the *Standard Installation* by pressing **Enter**, a screen will appear. You can also change the suggested directories here if you wish. Reply **N**o to this question.

(7) The installation checks if there is enough disk space available. Answer **Y**es to the question concerning continuation. You will then be asked about replacing existing files. This replacement is necessary for the smooth operation of the program and will not damage your other programs. The best thing to do is to press **Enter** to confirm. If you are

not sure, press **1** so that you will be asked each time any replacement is proposed.

(8) The AUTOEXEC.BAT file will probably have to be adapted. This will be beneficial so affirm by pressing **Enter**.

(9) If you wish to install additional graphic programs, answer the corresponding question with **Y**es. You must then select the required driver from the list. Otherwise press **Enter** and then **N**o.

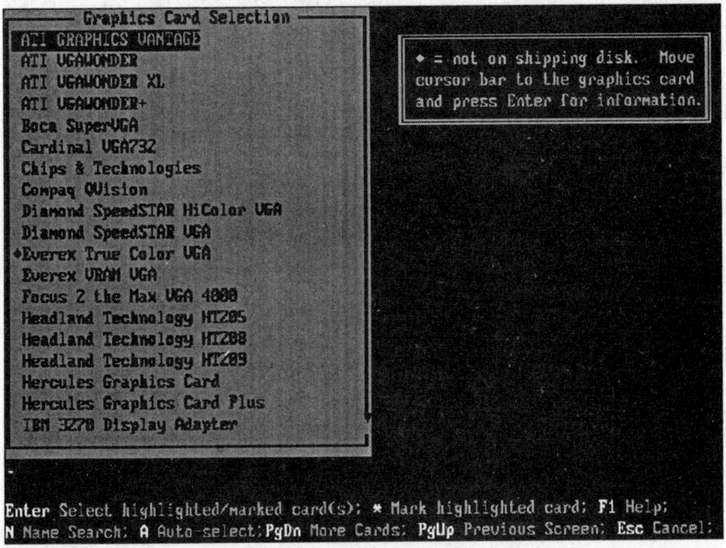

(10) You can move quickly through the pages of this list by pressing the **PgUp** and **PgDn** keys. But if you know the name of the driver you need, it is probably quicker to use the *Name Search* option to move to the required page. A more detailed description of this window is given below (point 11, printer driver installation).

(11) When you have selected the appropriate graphic driver, you can go on to select the required printer driver(s). If a printer is connected to your computer, answer **Y**es to this question and select the driver which corresponds to your printer. We shall

use the HP LaserJet as an example to illustrate the procedure.

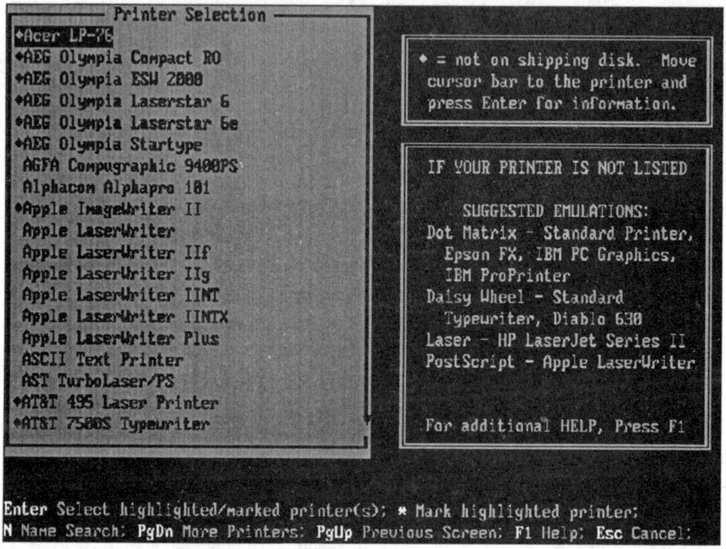

a) Select the *Name Search* option from the menu at the bottom of the screen by pressing **N**. Type the letter **H** in the *Name Search* box which appears. A list of printers beginning with the letter *H* appears immediately.
b) Use the Cursor Down key to move through the list until HP LaserJet is highlighted.
c) Confirm your choice by pressing **Enter** and reply **Y**es to the next question. The installation program may request an extra diskette. Insert this diskette in the disk drive if necessary.
d) Reply **N**o to the next question if you do not wish to install additional printer drivers.

The program installation is now continued. Insert the required diskettes into the disk drive at the appropriate times.

Note
It is also possible to install additional printer drivers at a later date. To do so, select the *Print/Fax* option from the *File* menu. The choose the *Select* option and *Add*.

15.2 Default settings

In general, you can begin working with WordPerfect without first having to alter the default settings. But altering these does allow you to adjust WordPerfect to your own particular requirements. Accordingly, we shall give a brief outline of how to adapt these settings.

Start up WordPerfect and select the *Setup* option from the *File* menu.

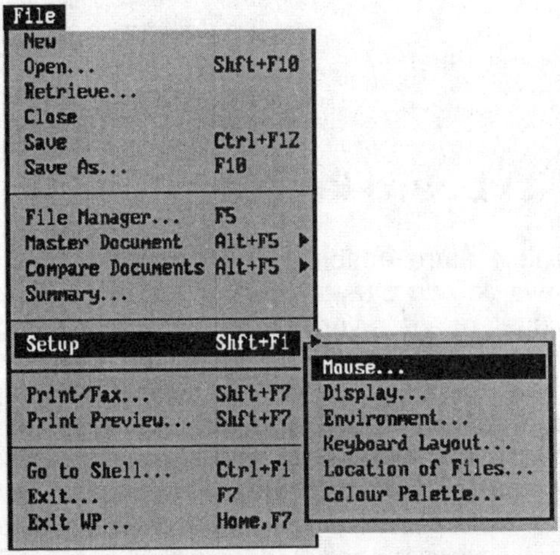

Option and function

Mouse	As the name indicates, this option is used to select the mouse driver. It is also used to set the double click speed, the acceleration rate and reversed usage for left-handed people if desired.

Display	This option is used to adjust the screen display settings, such as colour and resolution.
Environment	This option provides opportunity to change all kinds of WordPerfect default settings, such as Backup Options, Cursor Speed, Hyphenation etc.
Keyboard Layout	This option enables you to select a different keyboard definition, or change the significance of certain keys such as the function keys for instance.
Location of Files	This option enables you to specify the location of utility programs such as Hyphenation, Spelling Check, Thesaurus etc. Specify the drive and the directory here.
Colour Palette	This option determines the settings for the colour printer.

15.3 Keyboard layout

This feature enables you to redefine what individual keys do and thus tailor the keyboard to your own individual needs. WordPerfect is normally supplied with various definitions geared to certain situations. Windows adepts, when working with WordPerfect for DOS, can adapt the keyboard to the settings which largely correspond to those in the Windows version of WordPerfect (CUAWWPW52.WPK). These settings are stored in separate files with the extension .WPK. The significance of the keys depend on the keyboard definition you have chosen.

15.3.1 Selection of a keyboard definition

You can select a new keyboard definition as follows:

(1) Select the *Setup* option from the *File* menu and the choose *Keyboard Layout*. All the currently available options appear in a dialog box. The keyboard definition currently in use is marked with an asterisk.

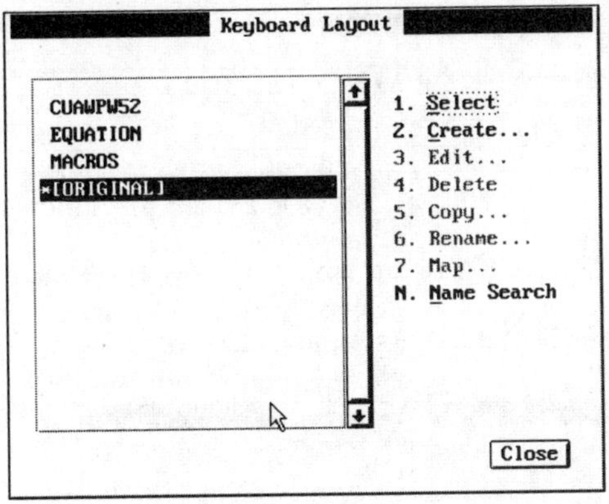

(2) Mark the required keyboard definition and choose *Select*.

The new keyboard definition is selected and the dialog window is closed. The new definition remains in force until a different definition is installed.

15.3.2 Defining the keyboard layout

You can also create your own new keyboard layout. Imagine that you have a regular correspondence with people in France. It would be very handy to have the letter é on your keyboard because it is often in use. By way of example we shall create a layout so that you can produce this letter by typing the key combination Ctrl-e. (You can of course make any letter of your own choice, such as the Spanish ñ for instance using the key combination Ctrl-n). This is how you do it:

(1) Select the *Setup* option from the *File* menu. Then select *Keyboard Layout*. Select option 2, *Create*, in the subsequent dialog window.
(2) Now enter a name in the *Keyboard Name* box. Type 'French' and conclude by pressing *Enter.*

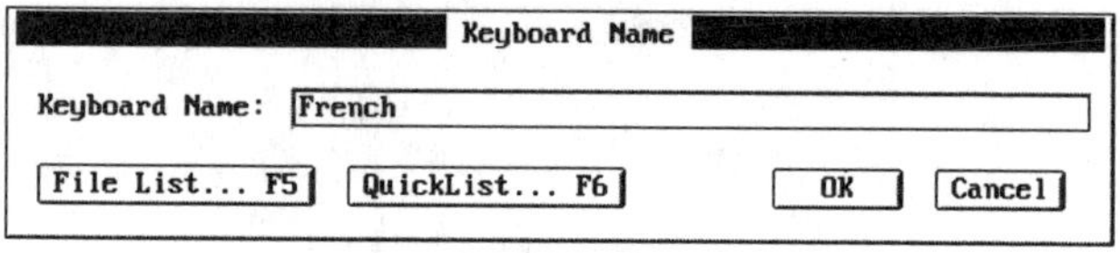

The *Edit Keyboard* dialog window appears.

(3) Select the first option, *Create*.

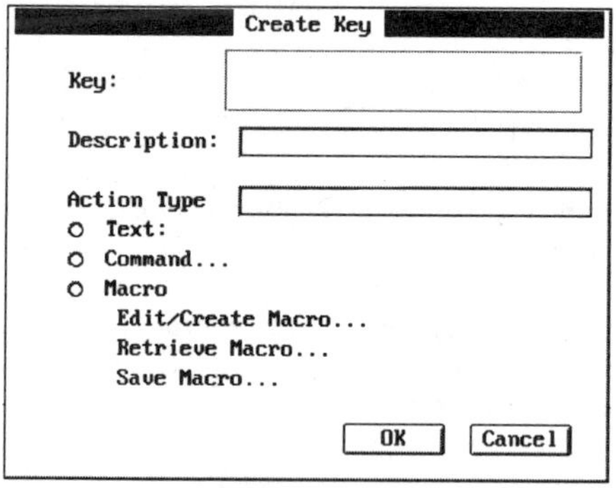

You can now begin defining the keys.

(4) Press the key combination Ctrl-e when the cursor is in the *Key* box and then press the letter D to move to the *Description* box. Type a brief outline of the function of this key there, such as 'E accent'. Press the Cursor Down key. The Text button is activated. Press **Enter** and then type the required key combination in the *Action Type* box. We have looked up the ASCII table in Appendix C and we have seen that the character we want is Alt-130.

Type this combination by holding down the Alt key and typing the numbers using the numeric keypad at the right of the keyboard. Then press **Enter** twice. The *Edit Keyboard* window appears.

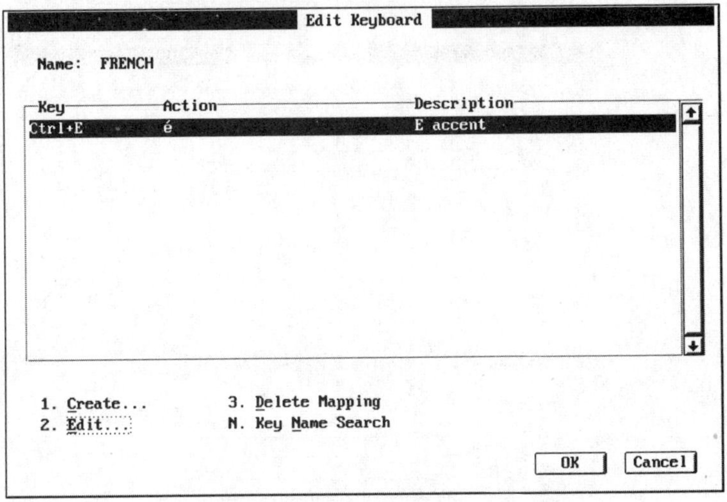

(5) Press **Tab** so that **OK** is selected and then press **Enter** to confirm. You can of course click directly on the **OK** button.

(6) You will return to the *Keyboard Layout* window. The French keyboard has been added to the list. If you now activate it by highlighting it and clicking on the first option, *Select*, your keyboard definition will come into force. Try it by pressing **Ctrl-e**.

We have given an example using one key. You can go on to make as many more alterations to the keyboard as you wish. You can always return to the original settings by going to the *Keyboard Layout* window and selecting *[ORIGINAL]*.

Appendix A

Character sets

When working with WordPerfect, you can make many more characters than are shown on the keyboard. The *WP Characters* option from the *Font* menu provides the following character sets in addition to the standard ASCII character set:

- Multinational
- Phonetic
- Box Drawing
- Typographic Symbols
- Iconic Symbols
- Maths/Scientific
- Maths/Sci. Extended
- Greek
- Hebrew
- Cyrillic
- Japanese
- User-Defined
- Arabic
- Arabic Script.

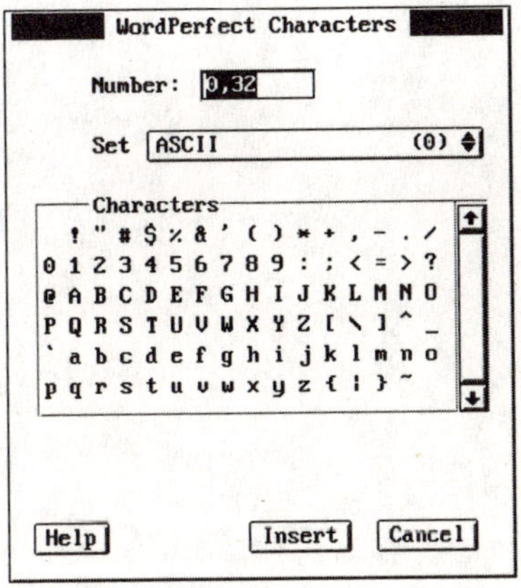

If you wish to use a symbol from one of these character sets, select the *WP Characters* option from the *Font* menu (the shortcut key combination is Ctrl-w).

When the *WordPerfect Characters* window appears on the screen, press the Cursor Down key or click on *Set*. The list of character sets is opened. Click on the set you want or highlight it by moving the cursor keys and then press **Enter**. Then click on *Insert* or press *I*. Whether or not the corresponding character actually can be printed depends on the capabilities of the connected printer.

Appendix B
Summary of commands

WordPerfect was originally a program which was operated using the keyboard. However, in versions 5 and 6, menu-driven operation has increased dramatically in significance. Nevertheless, many commands and functions can be implemented quickly and easily by means of keys and key combinations. The list below is a summary of the most important commands which can be executed using key commands on a keyboard under standard definition.

Adjacent Windows	Ctrl-F3,1,4
Append Block to File	Ctrl-F4,1,4
Backup	Shift-F1,3,1
Binding Offset	Shift-F8,7,9,2
Block, Append	Ctrl-F4,4
Block, Centre	Shift-F6
Block, Define	Alt-F4
Block, Delete	Ctrl-F4,3
Block, Delete	Del/Backspace
Block, Mark	Alt-F4
Block, Move	Ctrl-F4,1,Move Cursor,Enter
Block, Protect	Alt-F4,Shift-F8,7,1
Block, Right Align	Alt-F6
Block, Save in File	F10
Block, Sort	Ctrl-F9
Bold	F6 or Ctrl-B
Borders	Alt-F9,3
Box	Alt-F9
Calculate	Alt-F7,3
Cancel	Esc
Capital/Small Letters	Alt-F4,Shift-F3
Case Conversion	Alt-F4, Shift-F3
Centring	Shift-F6

Character Sets	Ctrl-W
Codes	F11
Columns	Alt-F7
Comment	Ctrl-F7,2
Control Printer	Shift-F7,6
Copy	Ctrl-C
Copy and Paste	Ctrl-Ins
Cut	Ctrl-X
Cut and Paste	Ctrl-Del
Date	Shift-F5
Delete Word	Ctrl-Backspace or Ctrl-Del
DOS command	Ctrl-F1,6
DOS, go to	Ctrl-F1,1
Double Underline	Ctrl-F8,3,3
Error Messages, Help	F1, Error Messages
Exit Document	F7
Exit WP	Home-F7
File Manager	F5
File, Open	Shift-F10
Footnote	Ctrl-F7,1
Font	Ctrl-F8
Fonts, Setup	Ctrl-F8,Shift-F1
Font Relative Size	Ctrl-F8,4
Grammatik	Alt-F1,3
Graphic	Alt-F9
Graphic Mode	Ctrl-F3,3
Go To Page	Ctrl-Home
Hard Page Break	Ctrl-Enter
Hard Space	Home-Spacebar
Headers	Shift-F8,5,1
Help	F1
Hypertext	Alt-F5,6
Image, Importing	Alt-F9, Shift-F10
Indent	F4
Indent First Line	Shift-F8,2,7

Indent Left and Right	Shift-F4
Insert Date Code	Shift-F5,2
Italics	Ctrl-I
Justification	Shift-F8,1,2
Kerning	Shift-F8,7,9,3
Keyboard Layout	Shift-F1,4
Line Draw	Ctrl-F3,5
Line Spacing	Shift-F8,1,3
Location of Files	Shift-F1,5
Macro, Record	Ctrl-F10
Macro, Play	Alt-F10
Margins, Document	Shift-F8,2
Margins, Paragraph	Shift-F8,2
Mark Page	Ctrl-F4,3
Mark Paragraph	Ctrl-F4,2
Mark Text	Alt-F5,1
Merge	Ctrl-F9,1
Merge Codes	Shift-F9
Mouse	Shift-F1,1
Open File	Shift-F10
Outline	Ctrl-F5
Page Borders	Shift-F8,3,B
Page Display Mode	Ctrl-F3,4
Page Format	Shift-F8,3
Page Numbering	Shift-F8,3,1
Paper Sizes	Shift-F8,3,4
Paragraph Borders	Shift-F8,1,5
Password	F10,F8
Paste	Ctrl-V
Print	Shift-F7
Printer, Select	Shift-F7,6
Retrieve Image	Alt-F9,Shift-F10
Right-Alignment	Alt-F6
Save Interim	F10

Search and Replace	Alt-F2
Search Backwards	Shift-F2
Search Forwards	F2
Select Block	F12 or Alt-F4
Select Page	Ctrl-F4,3
Select Paragraph	Ctrl-F4,2
Select Printer	Shift-F7,6
Spelling Check	Ctrl-F2
Spreadsheet, Create Link	Alt-F7,5,2
Spreadsheet, Edit Link	Alt-F7,5,3
Strikeout	Ctrl-F8,3,9
Start Printing	Shift-F7,6,Go
Style List	Alt-F8
Subscript	Ctrl-F8,5,3
Superscript	Ctrl-F8,5,2
Tables	Alt-F7,2
Tables, Edit	Alt-F11
Tab Set	Ctrl-F11
Text Mode	Ctrl-F3,2
Text Box	Alt-F9,1,1,Y,Text Box,Select
Thesaurus	Alt-F1,2
Tile Window	Ctrl-F3,1,4
Typeover	Ins
Underline	F8
Undo	Ctrl-Z
Units of measure	Shift-F1,3,7
Window	Ctrl-F3,1
Writing Tools	Alt-F1

Appendix C

ASCII characters to 256

Here is a summary of the special characters you can enter by holding down the Alt key and at the same time typing the corresponding number on the numeric keypad on the right of your keyboard. If you type Alt-172, for example, the character 1/4 will appear on the screen.

Whether you can print all the characters which appear on the screen depends on the capabilities of your printer.

Dec	Hex	Chr	Dec	Hex	Chr	Dec	Hex	Chr	Dec	Hex	Chr
0	0		32	20		64	40	@	96	60	`
1	1	☺	33	21	!	65	41	A	97	61	a
2	2	☻	34	22	"	66	42	B	98	62	b
3	3	♥	35	23	#	67	43	C	99	63	c
4	4	♦	36	24	$	68	44	D	100	64	d
5	5	♣	37	25	%	69	45	E	101	65	e
6	6	♠	38	26	&	70	46	F	102	66	f
7	7	•	39	27	'	71	47	G	103	67	g
8	8	◘	40	28	(	72	48	H	104	68	h
9	9	○	41	29	)	73	49	I	105	69	i
10	A	◙	42	2A	*	74	4A	J	106	6A	j
11	B	♂	43	2B	+	75	4B	K	107	6B	k
12	C	♀	44	2C	,	76	4C	L	108	6C	l
13	D	♪	45	2D	–	77	4D	M	109	6D	m
14	E	♫	46	2E	.	78	4E	N	110	6E	n
15	F	☼	47	2F	/	79	4F	O	111	6F	o
16	10	►	48	30	0	80	50	P	112	70	p
17	11	◄	49	31	1	81	51	Q	113	71	q
18	12	↕	50	32	2	82	52	R	114	72	r
19	13	‼	51	33	3	83	53	S	115	73	s
20	14	¶	52	34	4	84	54	T	116	74	t
21	15	§	34	35	5	85	55	U	117	75	u
22	16	▬	54	36	6	86	56	V	118	76	v
23	17	↨	55	37	7	87	57	W	119	77	w
24	18	↑	56	38	8	88	58	X	120	78	x
25	19	↓	57	39	9	89	59	Y	121	79	y
26	1A	→	58	3A	:	90	5A	Z	122	7A	z
27	1B	←	59	3B	;	91	5B	[	123	7B	{
28	1C	∟	60	3C	<	92	5C	\	124	7C	¦
29	1D	↔	61	3D	=	93	5D	]	125	7D	}
30	1E	▲	62	3E	>	94	5E	^	126	7E	~
31	1F	▼	63	3F	?	95	5F	_	127	7F	⌂

Dec	Hex	Chr	Dec	Hex	Chr	Dec	Hex	Chr	Dec	Hex	Chr
128	80	Ç	160	A0	á	192	C0	└	224	E0	α
129	81	ü	161	A1	í	193	C1	┴	225	E1	β
130	82	é	162	A2	ó	194	C2	┬	226	E2	Γ
131	83	â	163	A3	ú	195	C3	├	227	E3	π
132	84	ä	164	A4	ñ	196	C4	─	228	E4	Σ
133	85	à	165	A5	Ñ	197	C5	┼	229	E5	σ
134	86	å	166	A6	ª	198	C6	╞	230	E6	µ
135	87	ç	167	A7	º	199	C7	╟	231	E7	τ
136	88	ê	168	A8	¿	200	C8	╚	232	E8	Φ
137	89	ë	169	A9	⌐	201	C9	╔	233	E9	Θ
138	8A	è	170	AA	¬	202	CA	╩	234	EA	Ω
139	8B	ï	171	AB	½	203	CB	╦	235	EB	δ
140	8C	î	172	AC	¼	204	CC	╠	236	EC	∞
141	8D	ì	173	AD	¡	205	CD	═	237	ED	ø
142	8E	Ä	174	AF	«	206	CE	╬	238	EE	∈
143	8F	Å	175	B0	»	207	CF	╧	239	EF	∩
144	90	É	176	B1	░	208	D0	╨	240	F0	≡
145	91	æ	177	B2	▒	209	D1	╤	241	F1	±
146	92	Æ	178	B3	▓	210	D2	╥	242	F2	≥
147	93	ô	179	B4	│	211	D3	╙	243	F3	≤
148	94	ö	180	B5	┤	212	D4	╘	244	F4	⌠
149	95	ò	181	B6	╡	213	D5	╒	245	F5	⌡
150	96	û	182	B7	╢	214	D6	╓	246	F6	÷
151	97	ù	183	B8	╖	215	D7	╫	247	F7	≈
152	98	ÿ	184	B9	╕	216	D8	╪	248	F8	°
153	99	Ö	185	BA	╣	217	D9	┘	249	F9	•
154	9A	Ü	186	BB	║	218	DA	┌	250	FA	·
155	9B	¢	187	BC	╗	219	DB	█	251	FB	√
156	9C	£	188	BD	╝	220	DC	▄	252	FC	ⁿ
157	9D	¥	189	BE	╜	221	DD	▌	253	FD	²
158	9E	₧	190	BF	╛	222	DE	▐	254	FE	■
159	9F	ƒ	191	C0	┐	223	DF	▀	255	FF	

Index

PRINTED IN THE EEC